Good Practice for Good Jobs in Early Childhood Education and Care

This work is published under the responsibility of the Secretary-General of the OECD. The opinions expressed and arguments employed herein do not necessarily reflect the official views of OECD member countries.

This document, as well as any data and any map included herein, are without prejudice to the status of or sovereignty over any territory, to the delimitation of international frontiers and boundaries and to the name of any territory, city or area.

Please cite this publication as:
OECD (2019), *Good Practice for Good Jobs in Early Childhood Education and Care*, OECD Publishing, Paris, https://doi.org/10.1787/64562be6-en.

ISBN 978-92-64-89724-3 (print)
ISBN 978-92-64-80038-0 (pdf)

The statistical data for Israel are supplied by and under the responsibility of the relevant Israeli authorities. The use of such data by the OECD is without prejudice to the status of the Golan Heights, East Jerusalem and Israeli settlements in the West Bank under the terms of international law.

Photo credits: Cover © LightField Studios/Shutterstock

Corrigenda to OECD publications may be found on line at: *www.oecd.org/about/publishing/corrigenda.htm*.
© OECD 2019

You can copy, download or print OECD content for your own use, and you can include excerpts from OECD publications, databases and multimedia products in your own documents, presentations, blogs, websites and teaching materials, provided that suitable acknowledgement of OECD as source and copyright owner is given. All requests for public or commercial use and translation rights should be submitted to *rights@oecd.org*. Requests for permission to photocopy portions of this material for public or commercial use shall be addressed directly to the Copyright Clearance Center (CCC) at *info@copyright.com* or the Centre français d'exploitation du droit de copie (CFC) at *contact@cfcopies.com*.

Acknowledgements

The report was prepared under the overall supervision of the OECD Secretary-General, Angel Gurría, and the OECD Chief of Staff and Sherpa to the G20, Gabriela Ramos.

The OECD Directorate for Employment, Labour, and Social Affairs (ELS) prepared this report under the senior leadership of Stefano Scarpetta (Director of ELS), Mark Pearson (Deputy Director of ELS), Monika Queisser (Senior Counsellor and Head of the OECD Social Policy Division) and Willem Adema (Senior Economist in the OECD Social Policy Division).

The report was written by Chris Clarke and Antonela Miho (OECD Social Policy Division), with valuable contributions by Valerie Frey (OECD Social Policy Division) and Arno Engel (OECD Directorate for Education and Skills). Kirsten Wendland, Juliane Stahl (both German Federal Ministry for Family Affairs, Senior Citizens, Women and Youth), Christopher Prinz (OECD Directorate for Employment, Labour, and Social Affairs) and Elizabeth Shuey (OECD Directorate for Education and Skills) made valuable comments and contributions throughout the drafting process. Liv Gudmundson prepared the report for publication, with Natalie Lagorce, Lucy Hulett and Alastair Wood providing further logistical, publication and communications support.

The financial support provided by the German Federal Ministry for Family Affairs, Senior Citizens, Women and Youth (BMFSFJ) for this project is gratefully acknowledged.

Executive summary

OECD countries face a persistent challenge in recruiting and retaining highly skilled Early Childhood Education and Care (ECEC) staff. Mindful of quality issues and the benefits that come with well-trained staff, OECD countries are increasingly demanding ECEC staff undertake extensive pre-service training and attain high-level qualifications before entering the sector. Many OECD countries have raised or revised minimum qualification requirements in recent decades. Several (e.g. France, Iceland and Italy) even require pre-primary teachers to hold master's level qualifications. In-service training and professional development activities for ECEC workers are also receiving increased attention.

At the same time, however, many countries are struggling to attract and keep skilled staff in the ECEC sector. Low wages, a lack of status and public recognition, poor working conditions, and limited opportunities for professional development all mean that careers in ECEC are too often seen as unattractive. Staff recruitment is frequently difficult, and retention just as much of a challenge. Especially when coupled with an ageing workforce and general growth in demand for ECEC, these recruitment issues mean that many OECD countries are facing substantial shortages of skilled ECEC staff.

What can countries do to build a highly qualified and well-trained ECEC workforce? What is the best route to increasing staff skills without exacerbating staff shortages? How can countries boost pay and working conditions in the context of limited resources? There is no single silver bullet for constructing a high-quality workforce. However, building on existing OECD work on ECEC (e.g. the *OECD Starting Strong* series, the *OECD Babies and Bosses* series, and previous *OECD Early Childhood Education and Care Policy Review*s) and drawing on the experience of countries across the OECD, this report recommends that countries consider the following policy options.

Attracting and recruiting highly-skilled staff

- Countries must engage in efforts to improve the status and attractiveness of ECEC as a career. Options for doing so include increasing qualification requirements for staff in at least some roles, running information campaigns, and improving wages. Where constrained by limited resources, countries may want to consider targeting wage increases at staff with particular characteristics and/or using wage increases to help achieve other strategic objectives, such as improving staff qualification levels.
- Countries looking to build a high-quality workforce also need to engage in efforts to boost staff qualifications. Raising minimum qualification requirements is one option, but does have downsides. To avoid short-term bottlenecks in the supply of qualified new entrants, countries may want to consider staggering the introduction of new minimum requirements or targeting requirement increases at staff in certain roles (e.g. centre leaders).
- Pre-service education and training systems should be accessible. Countries should ensure alternative entry pathways are in place for talented potential workers unwilling or unable to undergo lengthy pre-service training. This includes, for instance, entry routes for university graduates with degrees in unrelated fields and older workers with relevant professional experience from outside

- of ECEC (e.g. nurses, care workers). Countries may also want to consider providing students with financial support during pre-service training in ECEC.
- Practice as well as theory is important in pre-service training. Different countries place different emphasis on the role of practical experience in pre-service training. Countries without extensive practical placement schemes should consider expanding the role of practical experience and workplace-based learning in their pre-service training programmes.
- To promote quality and improve the supply of potential workers, countries should engage in stronger efforts to bring men into ECEC. Measures to improve the status of ECEC in general will help, but countries should also consider engaging in information and recruitment campaigns. Norway has found some success in using affirmative action in the hiring process, though such policies should serve only as a temporary measure in the transition to a more gender-balanced workforce.

Retaining and developing highly-skilled staff

- Strategies to keep skilled staff inside the ECEC sector are just as important for a high-quality workforce as measures to recruit new staff. Low pay is one factor often cited by workers considering leaving the sector, and efforts to boost wages in general are likely to help improve staff retention. In addition, however, countries should consider revising wage structures and/or engaging in measures that reward performance and development through improved pay.
- Countries should also engage in strategies to enhance working conditions. Improving regulatory standards, including by reducing minimum child-to-staff ratios, is one option open to countries, even though such a move is likely to place an additional burden on public budgets. Smaller class sizes are important for service quality and can help improve worker retention by, for instance, reducing stress among staff.
- Countries should also consider engaging in activities to promote in-service training and professional development opportunities. This is vital for quality, and may help boost sector-wide retention by, for example, enhancing professional identity and improving career satisfaction. Importantly, just providing the option of training is not enough; countries should also use strategies to promote and encourage staff participation. Mandating in-service training is one option; introducing measures that incentivise training (e.g. through wage boosts) is another.

Table of contents

Acknowledgements　3

Executive summary　4
    Attracting and recruiting highly-skilled staff　4
    Retaining and developing highly-skilled staff　5

1 Introduction and overview　8
    1.1. The ECEC workforce challenge　8
    1.2. Good policies for good jobs in early childhood education and care　11

2 Attracting and recruiting highly-skilled staff　14
    2.1. Main findings　14
    2.2. Improving the attractiveness of ECEC as a career　15
    2.3. Improving pre-service training and 'job-readiness'　21
    2.4. Bringing men into the ECEC workforce　27

3 Retaining and developing highly-skilled staff　32
    3.1. Main findings　32
    3.2. Improving pay and recognition　33
    3.3. Improving working conditions　35
    3.4. Encouraging in-service training and professional development　38

Annex A. Summary of pre-service training and minimum qualification requirements　42

References　43
    Notes　49

Figures

Figure 1.1. On average across the OECD, more than one in four pre-primary teachers is aged 50 or over　10
Figure 2.1. On average across OECD countries, 1.7% of 15-year-old students expect to work in ECEC – a larger share than for primary education, secondary education, and nursing　16
Figure 2.2. Pre-primary teachers often earn far less than they could elsewhere　18
Figure 2.3. In many OECD countries, at least in the public sector, pay for pre-primary teachers now matches pay for primary teachers　19
Figure 2.4. Few men hold ECEC jobs　28
Figure 2.5. Boys are far less likely than girls to expect a career in ECEC　29
Figure 3.1. Salary progression for pre-primary teachers varies across OECD countries　34

Figure 3.2. Most pre-primary teachers in the OECD spend more hours in direct contact with children than primary teachers — 37
Figure 3.3. Child-to-staff ratios in pre-primary education differ considerably across OECD countries — 38

Boxes

Box 1.1. ECEC staff shortages in Germany — 9
Box 1.2. Types of ECEC service and types of ECEC staff — 13
Box 2.1. Sweden's *Teacher Salary Boost* programme — 20
Box 2.2. New Zealand's *Pathways to the Future* strategic plan for ECEC — 23
Box 2.3. Practical placements in Denmark's initial ECEC teacher training programme — 24
Box 2.4. England's Early Years Professional Programme — 26
Box 2.5. Affirmative action to get men in ECEC in Norway — 30
Box 3.1. The *Child Care WAGE$ Initiative* and *Workforce Incentive Project* in the United States — 34
Box 3.2. The *Teacher Education and Compensation Helps* (T.E.A.C.H.) and the *Child-care Retention Incentive* (CRI) programmes in the United States — 40

Follow OECD Publications on:

 http://twitter.com/OECD_Pubs

 http://www.facebook.com/OECDPublications

 http://www.linkedin.com/groups/OECD-Publications-4645871

 http://www.youtube.com/oecdilibrary

 http://www.oecd.org/oecddirect/

1 Introduction and overview

Recruiting and retaining highly skilled staff is a long-standing challenge for the early childhood education and care (ECEC) sector. Motivated by a large and growing body of research linking staff skills and competencies with process quality[1] and child development, learning and well-being (OECD, 2012[1]; OECD, 2018[2]), OECD countries are increasingly demanding that ECEC staff be highly skilled and highly qualified. Several OECD countries have revised and/or raised minimum qualification requirements in ECEC in recent decades. Many are also placing increasing emphasis on in-service training and professional development for ECEC workers.

However, recruiting (and retaining) skilled ECEC staff is not straightforward. Many potential workers do not see ECEC as an attractive career choice, and efforts to bring skilled staff into the sector are often hampered by the low status of the profession and low pay on offer. Staff turnover rates are frequently high in ECEC, and it is common to find workers leaving the sector for better pay, conditions, and career prospects elsewhere. As a result, many OECD countries are facing staff shortages in ECEC, either now or in the near future (Litjens and Taguma, 2017[3]; Oberhuemer and Schreyer, 2018[4]).

This report, developed with support from the German Federal Ministry of Family Affairs, Senior Citizens, Women and Youth (BMFSFJ), reviews policies and strategies to improve ECEC staff recruitment and retention. Building on existing OECD work on ECEC – including, for instance, the *OECD Starting Strong* series, the *OECD Babies and Bosses* series, and previous *OECD Early Childhood Education and Care Policy Review*s – the Seepro-r Project (Oberhuemer and Schreyer, 2018[4]) and the wider research literature, the report explores what countries can do to build a high-quality ECEC workforce. It examines measures and initiatives aimed at attracting and recruiting talented workers, discusses options for promoting pre-service training and "job-readiness", and explores strategies for improving working conditions, staff satisfaction, and worker retention. It draws in particular on selected policy examples from Denmark, England, New Zealand, Norway, Sweden, and the United States.

The report starts with a brief overview of the workforce challenge facing OECD countries and a summary of the main findings emerging from the report. Section 2 focuses on recruitment. It reviews policies and initiatives to bring skilled staff into the ECEC sector, including strategies improve the attractiveness of ECEC as a career option, initiatives to recruit highly qualified staff, and options for encouraging men to enter ECEC. Section 3 turns to staff retention and development. It covers policies and initiatives to promote retention through improved pay, as well as strategies to improve working conditions and promote opportunities for in-service training, professional development, and career progression

1.1. The ECEC workforce challenge

Many OECD countries are facing a shortage of skilled staff in ECEC. Participation in ECEC is growing in almost all OECD countries (OECD, 2017[5]; 2018[6]), but the supply of highly skilled and highly qualified workers is often struggling to keep up. Germany provides one of the clearest examples (Box 1.1). There, the expansion of the ECEC guarantee in 2013 to all children aged one and over, combined with demographic developments, means that the number of children in ECEC is expected to rise substantially over the next decade or so and, with it, the need for more staff (Prognos, 2018[7]). One estimate suggests that Germany may need close to half a million new ECEC staff by 2030 (Box 1.1).

> ### Box 1.1. ECEC staff shortages in Germany
>
> Germany, as much as any other OECD country, is facing significant challenges in ECEC workforce recruitment and retention. In 2013, Germany widened its legal entitlement to a place in ECEC to all children age one and over. Together with steady increases in the birth rate (OECD, 2018[6]) and sustained growth in the share of mothers in paid work (OECD, 2018[6]), the expansion of the entitlement has led to a sharp increase in the use of ECEC. Between 2008 and 2018, the number of children using registered ECEC services in Germany increased by over 25%, from 1 565 000 to 2 024 000 (Destatis, 2018[8]). Estimates suggest this growth is likely to continue over the next decade or so (Prognos, 2018[7]).
>
> The expansion of ECEC participation, alongside other changes like the gradual shift to full-day provision, is putting huge pressure on ECEC staffing in Germany. Total staff numbers have risen in recent years, from 365 000 educational professionals in 2008 to 596 000 in 2018 (Destatis, 2018[8]). However, expected further growth in ECEC participation, combined with large numbers of staff due to retire in the coming years, mean that many more new workers will be needed over the next decade or so (Oberhuemer and Schreyer, 2018[4]). Estimates by the Swiss consultancy firm Prognos suggest that Germany may need as many as 372 000 additional ECEC staff by 2025, and a further 112 000 by 2030 (Prognos, 2018[7]). This far exceeds the number of new entrants expected to graduate from pre-service training programmes in ECEC over the same period (181 000 by 2025, and a further 104 000 by 2030), potentially leading to a shortfall of approximately 191 000 by 2025 and 200 000 by 2030 (Prognos, 2018[7]).

Other countries are also facing shortages of qualified ECEC workers. In France, for instance, a combination of cuts to staffing during the late-2000s and a high birth rate has led to a shortage of staff in both the care-oriented day care sector aimed at children under 3, and the pre-primary sector aimed at children over 3 (Oberhuemer and Schreyer, 2018[4]). In England, the recent expansion of the free ECEC entitlement for 3- and 4-year-olds with working parents from 15 to 30 hours per week is increasing demand for the number of ECEC workers (Oberhuemer and Schreyer, 2018[4]). Countries like Finland and Sweden too, are expecting staff shortages in the coming years (Oberhuemer and Schreyer, 2018[4]), despite the long history and well-established nature of their ECEC systems.

A number of factors contribute to the general shortage of skilled staff in ECEC. First, in many OECD countries, the ECEC workforce is ageing. On average across OECD countries, 28% of pre-primary teachers are now aged 50 or over, rising to over 50% in Italy (Figure 1.1). Less than 20% are aged less than 30, on average. Older workers bring knowledge and experience to the sector, but also signal a looming issue – an ageing workforce means large numbers of staff will soon need to be replaced following retirement (Litjens and Taguma, 2017[3]).

Second, and related to the above, in many countries the ECEC industry is struggling to attract sufficient numbers of skilled and qualified new entrants (Litjens and Taguma, 2017[3]) (Section 2). Several countries (e.g. England, Finland and Norway) are finding it difficult to encourage enough talented students to enrol on pre-service ECEC training schemes (Oberhuemer and Schreyer, 2018[4]; Engel et al., 2015[9]), and even once qualified, not all graduates go on to have long-term careers in the sector. Indeed, several studies find that many ECEC students intend to stay in the industry for only a limited time before moving on to other areas, such as primary teaching (Press, Wong and Gibson, 2015[10]; Moloney, 2015[11]).

Figure 1.1. On average across the OECD, more than one in four pre-primary teachers is aged 50 or over

Distribution of pre-primary education teachers by age group, 2016

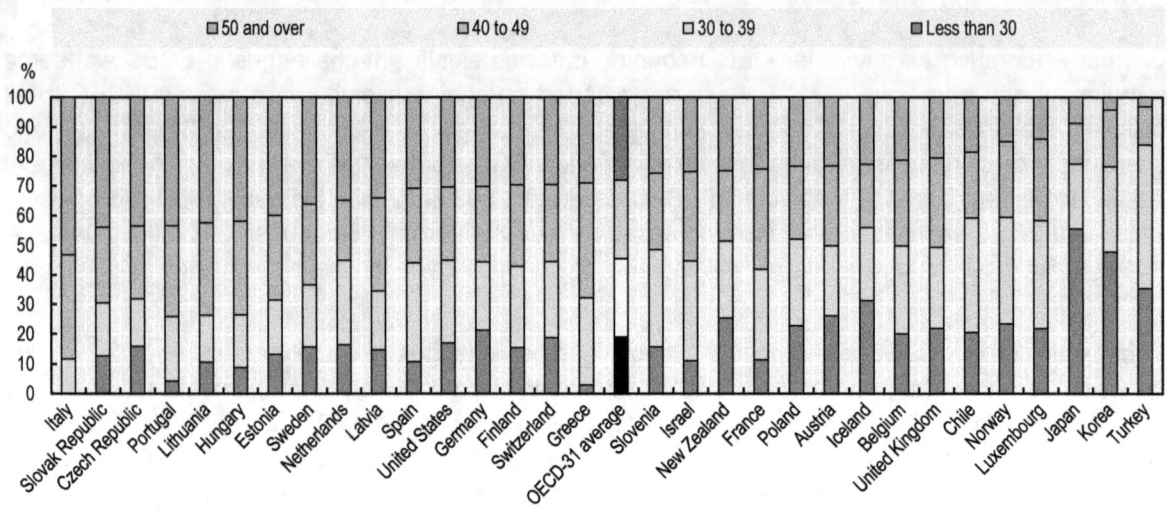

Note: 'Pre-primary education teachers' refers to teachers in pre-primary education (ISCED2011 level 0 programme 2). Data for Italy refer to 2012, for Estonia to 2014, and for New Zealand to 2015.
Source: *OECD Education Database*, http://www.oecd.org/education/database.htm, and *OECD Employment Database*, http://www.oecd.org/employment/emp/onlineoecdemploymentdatabase.htm.

Third, the ECEC sector often suffers from high staff turnover and poor worker retention (Section 3). There are few internationally comparable statistics on turnover in ECEC, but what data do exist tend to point to a common challenge in staff retention. Numbers from New Zealand, for example, show an ECEC teacher turnover rate of 19%, higher than the national average (MoE, 2014[12]). Estimates from the United States suggest the staff turnover rate in pre-primary education is 30%, and in the day-care sector as high as 35% (OECD, 2012[1]).

Fourth, across countries, the ECEC workforce is also overwhelmingly female (Section 2.4). On average across OECD countries, just 3% of pre-primary education teachers are men, and even in the best performing countries (e.g. France, the Netherlands and Norway) rates reach only around 7.5 to 12.5% (see Figure 2.4). The share of male staff is equally poor in services aimed at children under age 3. From a process quality and child outcome perspective, the limited number of men in ECEC has implications for child development, particularly in relation to the development of attitudes towards gender roles. On a staffing level, it also reduces the pool of available workers.

1.1.1. ECEC careers are too often seen as unappealing

Underlying all these issues is the fact that many potential and existing ECEC workers do not see a career in ECEC as appealing. Importantly, available evidence suggests the idea of working in ECEC is not necessarily unattractive in and of itself. Survey results from Germany, for example, show that as many as 5% of people aged 16 and over have at least once seriously considered a job in ECEC (IfD-Allensbach, 2018[13]). Data from OECD PISA 2015 suggest that 15-year-olds are actually more likely to say they expect a job in ECEC than in primary education, secondary education, or nursing (see Figure 2.1). However, various factors combine to make the reality of ECEC work often less attractive than in many competing occupations.

Low wages are one of the most frequently cited reasons for poor recruitment and retention (Sections 2.22.2.2 and 3.2). Many OECD countries have introduced measures aimed at boosting ECEC pay in recent years, especially in the pre-primary sector, but ECEC workers often still earn much less than they could elsewhere (see Figure 2.2). A lack of recognition and the perceived lack of status in ECEC work is another driver (Section2.2). ECEC staff often report finding their work valuable and rewarding (McDonald, Thorpe and Irvine, 2018[14]; Moloney, 2015[11]; Irvine et al., 2016[15]). At the same time, however, they also feel under-valued and under-rewarded for their efforts (Ackerman, 2006[16]; Irvine et al., 2016[15]). One study in Germany found that many staff (74%) are suffering from a "gratification crisis", whereby they believe the work they do greatly exceeds the recognition and rewards received (Schreyer et al., 2014[17]). Only 2% of respondents believe their work is fully appreciated in society (Schreyer et al., 2014[17]).

Working conditions also play a role (Section 3.3). Numerous studies highlight the importance of aspects of the work environment like organisational climate and child-to-staff ratios for process quality and child learning and development (OECD, 2018[2]), but these factors are also important for staff job satisfaction and worker retention. ECEC workers considering leaving their job often point to stress, exhaustion, and poor support as key drivers (Totenhagen et al., 2016[18]). Promoting better working conditions by, for example, reducing class size and improving support structures can help increase staff performance, satisfaction, and retention (OECD, 2012[1]; OECD, 2018[2]).

Staff education and training systems are important too (see sections 2.3 and 3.4). Comprehensive education and training – both pre-service and in-service – is crucial for the construction of a high-quality workforce, but may also hamper recruitment if systems are not flexible and responsive to the needs of potential new staff with different backgrounds. For example, pre-service training systems that demand staff attain a specific university-level qualification in ECEC before entry may deter skilled graduates with a degree in an unrelated subject, or older workers seeking a career change. Those that refuse to recognise relevant skills and knowledge gained outside of ECEC may exclude many talented workers with experience from elsewhere.

1.2. Good policies for good jobs in early childhood education and care

The following sections of this report cover policies and strategies to improve ECEC staff recruitment and retention. Cross-country differences in governance structures, modes of provision (e.g. public- or market-based), the political and economic climate, and the existing state of the ECEC workforce mean that certain measures may be more relevant to some countries than to others. Nonetheless, the main general policy messages emerging from the report include:

- As a first step, countries must engage in efforts to improve the attractiveness of ECEC as a career (Section2.2). This includes measures to improve the status of the profession through, for example, increased qualification requirements for staff in at least some roles, as well as initiatives to improve wages. Where constrained by limited resources, countries may want to consider targeting wage increases at staff with particular characteristics and/or using wage increases to help achieve other strategic objectives. New Zealand's cost-based supply-side funding system, which has helped increase the number of qualified and registered staff in ECEC, provides one example.

- In tandem with measures to improve status and pay, countries looking to build a high-quality workforce also need to engage in efforts to boost staff qualifications (Section 2.3). Raising minimum qualification requirements is one route to a highly qualified workforce, but does have drawbacks. To avoid short-term bottlenecks in the supply of qualified new entrants, countries may want to consider staggering the introduction of new minimum requirements or targeting requirement increases at staff in certain roles (e.g. centre leaders).

- Pre-service education and training systems should be accessible. Standard pre-service training programmes often last three, four or even five years in OECD countries, which may deter many new entrants. Countries should ensure alternative entry pathways are put in place for talented potential workers unwilling or unable to undergo lengthy pre-service training. This includes, for example, university graduates with a degree in an unrelated field, or older workers with relevant professional experience from outside of ECEC (e.g. nurses, care workers). England's Early Years Professional Programme, which helped bring many university graduates into the ECEC workforce, provides one such example. Countries may also want to consider providing students with financial support during pre-service training in ECEC.

- Practice as well as theory is important in pre-service education and training. Different countries place different emphasis on the role of practical experience in pre-service training, but evidence suggests it can be hugely beneficial for process quality and staff 'job-readiness'. Countries without extensive practical placement schemes should consider expanding the role of practical experience and workplace-based learning in their pre-service training programmes. In Denmark, for example, student ECEC teachers spend the equivalent of more than one year on practical placements.

- To promote process quality and improve the supply of potential workers, countries should engage in stronger efforts to bring men into ECEC (Section 2.4). Measures to improve the status of ECEC will help, but countries should also consider engaging in information and recruitment campaigns. Norway has found some success in using affirmative action in the hiring process, though such policies should serve only as a temporary measure in the transition to a more gender-balanced workforce.

- Policies to attract and recruit ECEC staff need to be matched by strategies to keep skilled staff inside the sector. Low pay is one factor often cited by workers considering leaving the sector, and efforts to boost wages in general are likely to help improve staff retention. In addition, however, countries should consider revising wage structures and/or engaging in measures that reward performance and development through improved pay (Section 3.2). Wage boost initiatives from the United States demonstrate how providing salary supplements based on education and professional development activities can help promote retention.

- Countries should also engage in strategies to enhance working conditions (Section 3.3). Improving regulatory standards, including by reducing minimum child-to-staff ratios, is one option open to countries, even though such a move places an additional burden on public budget. Smaller class sizes are important for service quality and can help improve worker retention by, for instance, reducing stress among staff.

- Countries should also consider engaging in activities to promote in-service training and professional development opportunities (Section 3.4). This is vital for process quality, and may help boost sector-wide retention (through e.g. enhancing professional identity and improving career satisfaction), even though there is some evidence to suggest in-service training might increases the likelihood of staff changing specific jobs. Importantly, just providing the option of training is not enough; countries should also use strategies to promote and encourage staff participation. Mandating in-service training is one option. Introducing measures that incentivise training – such as the offer of wage boosts for participating staff, as used in programmes the U.S. states of Wisconsin and California – is another.

> **Box 1.2. Types of ECEC service and types of ECEC staff**
>
> **Types of ECEC services**
>
> The types of ECEC services available to children and parents vary considerable across countries. However, most ECEC settings typically fall into one of the following categories:
>
> - Regular centre-based ECEC: More formalised ECEC centres typically belong to one of these three sub-categories:
>   - Centre-based ECEC for children from the age of 3: Often called pre-primary education, kindergarten or pre-school, these settings tend to be more formalised and are often linked to the education system.
>   - Centre-based ECEC for children under the age of 3: Often called day care, crèche, or nursery school, these settings may have an educational function, but are typically attached to the social or welfare sector and often put greater emphasis on care. These services are sometimes provided in schools or alongside services for older children, but are also often provided in designated day care centres.
>   - Age-integrated centre-based ECEC for children from birth or age 1 up to the beginning of primary school: Called kindergarten, pre-school, or pre-primary, these settings offer a holistic pedagogical provision of education and care. They are often offered on a full-day basis.
> - Family child care: Licensed home-based ECEC, which is most prevalent for children under age 3. These settings may or may not have an educational function and be part of the regular ECEC system. These services are traditionally provided in a home setting. This can be at the provider's home or at the child's own home.
> - Licensed or formalised drop-in ECEC centres: Often receiving children across the entire ECEC age bracket and even beyond, these drop-in centres allow parents to complement home-based care by family members or family childcare with more institutionalised services on an ad-hoc basis.
>
> **Types of ECEC staff**
>
> There are also a variety of categories of professionals working in ECEC systems, and job titles are diverse across countries. Broadly, most staff fall into one of the following categories:
>
> - Teachers and comparable practitioners: Most often found in pre-primary education services and age-integrated centre based services. Pre-primary education teachers have the most responsibility for a group of children at the class or playroom level. They may also be called pedagogue, educator, childcare practitioner or pedagogical staff in pre-primary education.
> - Child care workers: Most often found in the care-oriented day care sector aimed at children under age 3. They also often called day care workers.
> - Family and domestic care workers: Family and domestic care workers are caregivers working in family child care or home-based care settings. Often also known as childminders or nannies.
> - Assistants and support staff: Assistants support the teacher in a group of children or class. Assistants are more common in ECEC than in e.g. primary education. They usually have lower qualification requirements than teachers, which may range from no formal requirements to, for instance, vocational education and training.
>
> Sources: (OECD, 2017[5]; 2018[19]; 2018[6]).

2 Attracting and recruiting highly-skilled staff

Recruiting skilled staff is a persistent challenge for ECEC. Mindful of quality issues, OECD countries are increasingly demanding new staff are highly qualified, but these efforts are hampered by low wages and a perception that ECEC is unattractive as a career (Thorpe et al., 2011[20]). Pre-service training systems, while vital for staff competencies and process quality (OECD, 2018[2]), may also restrict the number of new entrants if they are not sufficiently flexible and responsive to the needs of potential new staff with different backgrounds. Making ECEC an appealing career choice and boosting the number of skilled staff entering the sector requires competitive pay and career prospects and a flexible and high-quality education and training system.

This section reviews policies and initiatives to recruit highly skilled staff. It starts with an overview of measures aimed at improving the attractiveness of ECEC as a career. Topics covered include options to promote the professional standing of ECEC, initiatives to boost wages and salaries, and campaigns to attract staff and increase public awareness of ECEC careers. The second sub-section covers policies and initiatives for boosting pre-service training and the 'job-readiness' of new ECEC staff. It looks at raising minimum qualification requirements, measures to introduce practical work experience into the training process, and options for providing alternative pathways into the sector. The third and final sub-section discuss initiatives looking to encourage men to enter the ECEC sector. It covers campaigns to increase the awareness and acceptance of ECEC as a career option for men, male worker support and networking initiatives, and affirmative action policies favouring male candidates.

2.1. Main findings

- Countries must engage in efforts to improve the status and attractiveness of ECEC as a career. Options for doing so include increasing qualification requirements for staff in at least some roles, and improving wages. Where constrained by limited resources, countries may want to consider targeting wage increases at staff with particular characteristics and/or using wage increases to help achieve other strategic objectives.
- Countries looking to build a high-quality workforce also need to engage in efforts to boost staff qualifications. Raising minimum qualification requirements is one option, but does have downsides. To avoid short-term bottlenecks in the supply of qualified new entrants, countries may want to consider staggering the introduction of new minimum requirements or targeting requirement increases at staff in certain roles (e.g. centre leaders).
- Pre-service education and training systems should be accessible. Countries should ensure alternative entry pathways are in place for talented potential workers unwilling or unable to undergo lengthy pre-service training. This includes entry routes for, for instance, university graduates with a degree in an unrelated field, and older workers with relevant professional experience from outside

of ECEC (e.g. nurses, care workers). Countries may also want to consider providing students with financial support during pre-service training in ECEC.
- Practice as well as theory is important in pre-service training. Different countries place different emphasis on the role of practical experience in pre-service training. Countries without extensive practical placement schemes should consider expanding the role of practical experience and workplace-based learning in their pre-service training programmes.
- To promote process quality and improve the supply of potential workers, countries should engage in stronger efforts to bring men into ECEC (Section 2.4). Measures to improve the status of ECEC will help, but countries should also consider engaging in information and recruitment campaigns. Norway has found some success in using affirmative action in the hiring process, though such policies should serve only as a temporary measure in the transition to a more gender-balance workforce.

2.2. Improving the attractiveness of ECEC as a career

Countries across the OECD are struggling to attract the skilled and motivated ECEC staff they need. Information from the SEEPRO-R project – a Europe-wide study of the ECEC workforce funded by the Federal Ministry of Family Affairs, Senior Citizens, Women and Youth (BMFSFJ) – suggests that a majority of European countries face ECEC staff shortages, either now or in the near future (Oberhuemer and Schreyer, 2018[4]). In England, estimates by Ceeda – a private sector research agency specialising in early years research – suggest that in summer 2017 there were approximately 25 000 staff vacancies in the private and voluntary sector, equivalent to almost 10% of the existing workforce (Ceeda, 2018[21]). In Germany, changes in policy combined with demographic and economic factors mean that as many as 372 000 additional ECEC staff may be needed by 2025, and a further 112 000 by 2030 (Prognos, 2018[7]). These estimates far exceed the expected number of new entrants graduating from pre-service training programmes over the same period (181 000 by 2025, and a further 104 000 by 2030) (Prognos, 2018[7]). Even in Sweden, where the ECEC industry is well-established and jobs are comparatively well-paid (see Figure 2.2 and Figure 2.3), the government is anticipating teacher shortages in the coming years, largely on account of demographic changes and an ageing workforce (Oberhuemer and Schreyer, 2018[4]).

The problem is not that working with young children is seen as unappealing in itself. Many adolescents – especially adolescent girls – express an interest in a career in early childhood education and care. In 2015, the OECD's Programme for International Student Assessment (PISA) asked 15-year-old students "*What kind of job do you expect to have when you are about 30 years old?*" On average across OECD countries, 1.7% responded that they expect to work in an occupation related to ECEC (Figure 2.1). This is a lower share than for some of the most popular occupations, such as working as a doctor (6.6%, on average) or an architect or designer (4.1%), but higher than competing occupations like nursing (1.6%) and primary (1.2%) and secondary teaching (1.5%) (Figure 2.1). All too often, however, this early enthusiasm fails to translate into a decision to enter an ECEC career. Several countries (e.g. Finland, Norway) are struggling to attract enough talented students onto pre-service ECEC training schemes (Oberhuemer and Schreyer, 2018[4]; Engel et al., 2015[9]). In England, at the start of the 2018-19 academic year, there were approximately 35 times *fewer* students entering early years initial teacher training (365) than there were entering primary education initial teacher training (12 975) (DfE, 2018[22]).[2] And even when people do choose to study for a qualification in ECEC, there is no guarantee that they are anticipating a life-long career in the sector. Indeed, several studies find that many ECEC students intend to stay in the industry for only a limited time before moving on to other areas, such as primary teaching (Press, Wong and Gibson, 2015[10]; Moloney, 2015[11]). To attract the motivated and highly skilled staff it needs, the ECEC sector needs to become more attractive as a career and as a profession. This involves improving status, boosting pay, and softening barriers to entry for potential new staff.

2.2.1. Promoting the status of ECEC jobs

Compared to competing occupations such as nursing and primary and secondary teaching, jobs in early childhood education and care often suffer from a lack of status and recognition. All too often, ECEC work is seen by the public as a vocation rather than a profession, and careers in ECEC as low status with only limited appeal (OECD, 2012[1]; Litjens and Taguma, 2017[3]). For example, one focus group-based study in New Zealand found that although teaching as a whole was regarded as a comparatively low-status profession, early childhood teaching was afforded lower status than primary teaching and, in turn, secondary teaching (Hall and Langton, 2006[23]). ECEC staff themselves also consistently report feeling under-valued and under-appreciated (Irvine et al., 2016[15]; Press, Wong and Gibson, 2015[10]).

In many cases, the low status of the sector is likely related to the perception that ECEC work is low- or unskilled (Ackerman, 2006[16]). As with many other occupations traditionally regarded as 'women's work', the skills and talents of ECEC staff are often under-valued. This is particularly the case for the care-oriented day care sector aimed at children under age 3 (Litjens and Taguma, 2017[3]). In Hall and Langton's focus group study, justifications for respondents' low regard for ECEC work included beliefs that ECEC teachers undergo shorter training and have a less difficult job than their counterparts in higher levels of education (Hall and Langton, 2006[23]). Notably, respondents also pointed to the fact that ECEC staff are less likely to be men.

Figure 2.1. On average across OECD countries, 1.7% of 15-year-old students expect to work in ECEC – a larger share than for primary education, secondary education, and nursing

Percentage of 15-year-old students who expect to work in the given occupation when they are age 30, selected occupations, OECD average, 2015

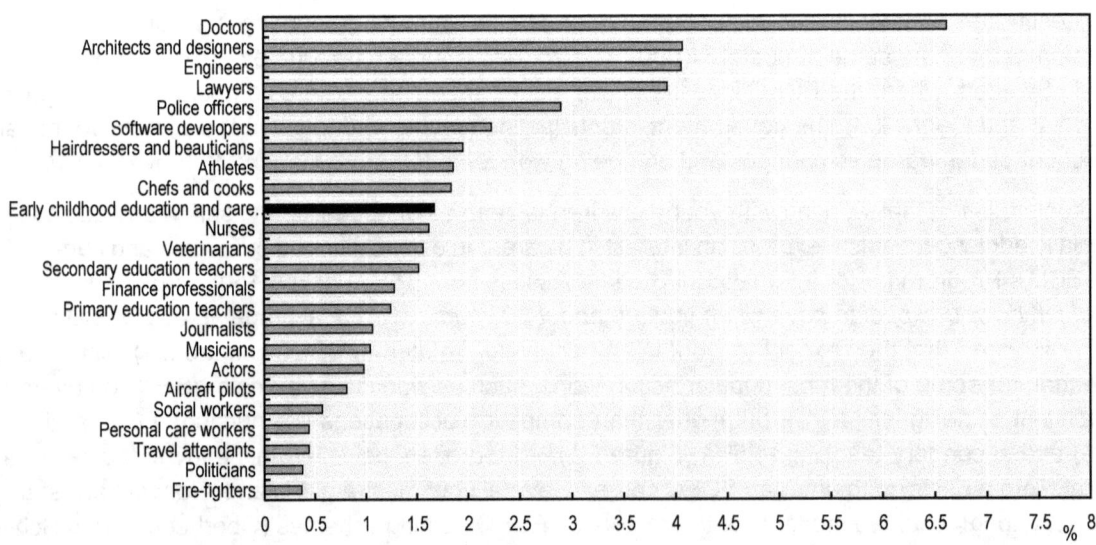

Note: 15-year-old students were asked "What kind of job do you expect to have when you are about 30 years old?" Answers to the question were coded using the ISCO-08 (International Standard of Classification of Occupations) classification of occupations at the 4-digit level. Students who expect to work in "early childhood education and care" are those with answers coded under ISCO-08 groups 2342 ("Early childhood educators") or 5311 ("Child care workers"). On average across OECD countries, an additional 0.15% gave answers that were coded under the broader ISCO-08 groups 234 ("Primary school and early childhood teachers") or 531 ("Child care workers and teachers' aides") but could not be further defined. These students are not included in the figure.
Source: OECD calculations based on the OECD Programme for International Student Assessment (PISA) 2015 Database, http://www.oecd.org/pisa/.

Currently, minimum qualification requirements in ECEC differ across countries and service types (see Section 2.3). Requirements for pre-primary teachers are often now comparable to those for primary teachers, but those for staff in the care-oriented sector for children under age 3 are frequently still low (OECD, 2014[24]; OECD, 2012[1]). Indeed, in several OECD countries, many day care staff continue to hold only low-level formal qualifications – in England, for example, almost 20% of staff in group-based day care settings hold less than an upper-secondary level qualification (DfE, 2018[25]). In other countries, ECEC staff undergo extensive pre-service training but the qualifications themselves carry less prestige than those for competing occupations. In Germany, for instance, pre-primary teachers are trained at the vocational level rather than at university level, as is the case for primary and secondary teachers (OECD, 2014[24]). Raising qualification requirements and/or using university-accredited programmes for pre-service training for at least some staff (see Section 2.3.1) has the potential to boost the professional status of ECEC teachers.

However, not all staff need to be educated to university level before entering the sector (Section 2.3.1). Attaining university-level qualifications is costly and can act as a barrier to entry for potential staff (see Section 2.3). Moreover, many existing but unqualified staff already have extensive knowledge and skills. For these staff, a more appropriate course of action may be to introduce awards that signal and recognise *existing* competencies. As just one example, Australia operates a "Recognition of Prior Learning" (RPL) programme whereby existing skills, knowledge and experience gained through working and learning can be used as credits counting towards a vocational ECEC qualification (DoET, 2017[26]). This helps experienced but unqualified staff have their skills recognised and allows early childhood workers to become qualified ECEC professionals without needing to undertake a full ECEC training programme. New Zealand also operates a similar programme (MoE, 2018[27]).

Another option is to use media and campaigns to increase public recognition of ECEC work and attract staff to the sector. For example, between 2012 and 2014, Norway ran a national recruitment campaign named "*The Best Job in the World is Vacant*", with the aim of raising the status of ECEC teaching and bringing new workers into ECEC pre-service training (Engel et al., 2015[9]). The campaign established regional networks, tasked with developing local measures. One of these local networks (in Oslo and Arkeshus) participated in education fairs and organised career days for trainee ECEC teachers (Engel et al., 2015[9]). In New Zealand, the Ministry of Education has put considerable effort into promoting ECEC on its public-facing website (MoE, 2019[28]). One section of the website is dedicated to parents and the public, informing them about the benefits of ECEC and the skills of ECEC staff. The aim is to educate and raise the profile of early childhood education and care, and to elevate the status of ECEC teachers (Litjens and Taguma, 2017[3]). Other campaign examples for teaching in the wider education sector include Estonia's "Study to Become a Teacher" campaign, which features videos of celebrities recalling their memories of school and of teachers explaining why their enjoy their jobs; France's "Ambition teach" (*Ambition Enseigner*) and "The school changes with you" (*L'école change avec vous*) television advertising campaign; and England's "Get into Teaching" website, which aims to attract staff to the sector and provides information and advice on training and careers (DfE, 2019[29]).

2.2.2. Improving wages and rewards

Related to the low status of the profession, wages and salaries in ECEC have historically been and, in many cases, continue to be very low. This is especially the case for staff working in care-oriented services aimed at very young children under age 3. In the United States, for instance, the mean annual wage for a child day care worker is USD 22 190, which fits easily into the bottom quarter of the wage distribution (BLS, 2017[30]). But even in the pre-primary sector, pay is often relatively often low. In Germany, for example, salaries for pre-primary teachers vary considerably with the relevant collective agreement[3] but are typically much lower than for competing occupations, such as primary education teaching (Oberhuemer and Schreyer, 2018[4]). Across countries, despite their relative advantage within the sector, pre-primary teachers continue to earn far less than similarly educated workers employed elsewhere (Figure 2.2).

Figure 2.2. Pre-primary teachers often earn far less than they could elsewhere

Average annual actual salaries of teachers in public pre-primary institutions relative to the annual earnings of workers with similar educational attainment (weighted average), 25- to 64-year-olds, 2016 or latest available year

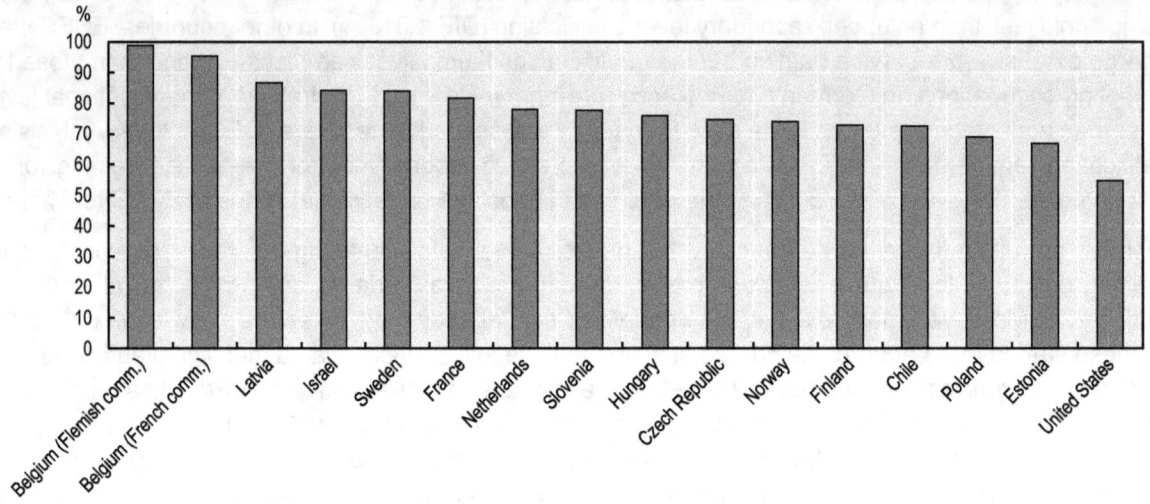

Note: Data for France and the Netherlands refer to 2014, and for Chile, the Czech Republic, Finland, and Belgium refer to 2015.
Source: *OECD Education at a Glance 2018*, http://www.oecd.org/education/education-at-a-glance/. .

Low wages damage the ECEC sector's efforts to recruit new staff (Ackerman, 2006[16]). It is not just that potential recruits may *prefer* to work in better paying occupations; for many, the low wages on offer in ECEC act as a firm barrier to a career the sector. Evidence from a staff survey in Australia suggests many ECEC workers are only able to continue in their position because their partner or other family members 'subsidise' their wages by contributing a disproportionate share to household expenses (Irvine et al., 2016[15]). Studies from other countries (e.g. England) show that ECEC staff are often in a position of high financial insecurity (Bonetti, 2019[31]). For talented workers who cannot (or do not want to) draw on others for financial assistance, low pay means a job in ECEC is likely to be ruled out in favour of higher-paying alternatives.

Many OECD countries are making efforts to increase pay for ECEC workers, especially at the pre-primary level. It is increasingly common for countries to align wages for pre-primary teachers with those for teachers in primary education (Litjens and Taguma, 2017[3]; OECD, 2017[32]). The Czech Republic, Hungary, Korea, Portugal, New Zealand and the Slovak Republic have all recently moved to ensure pay parity between pre-primary and primary teachers (Litjens and Taguma, 2017[3]). Today, in 19 OECD countries, statutory starting salaries for pre-primary teachers working in the public sector exactly match statutory starting salaries for primary teachers (Figure 2.3) ((OECD, 2017[32])). There is less evidence of a trend towards improved wages for workers in day care settings for children under age three, especially in countries that operate 'split systems', with day care services operated separately from pre-primary services.

Figure 2.3. In many OECD countries, at least in the public sector, pay for pre-primary teachers now matches pay for primary teachers

Annual statutory starting salaries for teachers' in public institutions, pre-primary education and primary education, USD PPP, 2017

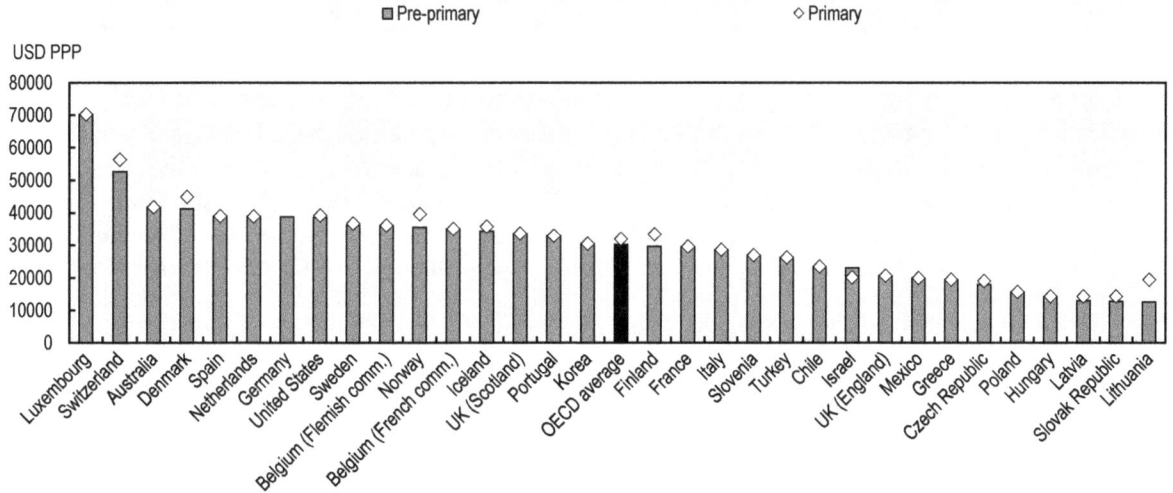

Note: Information refers to the statutory starting salary for someone entering the sector with the minimum required qualifications. For Finland, data on pre-primary teachers includes the salary of kindergarten teachers who are the majority. For Germany, statutory salaries vary considerably depending on collective bargaining agreement. The data shown refer to gross basic starting salary of a pre-primary teacher ("Erzieher") 'with demanding tasks' covered by the TVöD SuE collective agreement for workers in public social and educational services. For Luxembourg, data includes social security contributions and pension-scheme contributions paid by the employers. For New Zealand and Sweden, data exclude social security contributions and pension-scheme contributions paid by the employees. For Sweden and the United States, data refer to actual base salaries. The OECD average does not include Germany.
Source: OECD (2018), *OECD Education at a Glance 2018*, http://www.oecd.org/education/education-at-a-glance/; for Germany, OECD calculations based on information from Oberhuemer and Schreyer (2018[4])

Resource constraints for providers are a key challenge in improving ECEC staff pay. Depending on the exact nature of the system, service provider budgets are often constrained by limits (either statutory or practical) on the fees that can be charged to parents and/or by the level of subsidies received from public bodies. Staff salaries generally represent the single largest operating cost for providers, and even modest increases in wages are likely require to huge resources.

While it might be preferable to improve wages for most if not all ECEC staff, one option in the face of resource constraints is to target wage supplements at staff with particular qualifications or characteristics or to use wage increases to help with other strategic objectives. New Zealand, for example, has since 2005 operated a supply-side funding system that allocates greater resources to centres with greater numbers of qualified and registered ECEC teachers, with the aim of allowing services to offer improved wages to qualified staff (Box 2.2). Available evidence suggests the share of qualified and registered teachers in ECEC in New Zealand has doubled since its introduction (Box 2.2). Other examples include Korea – who, since 2012, have provided a wage boost to day care staff in centres delivering the 'Nuri curriculum', a standardised course of study for 3- to 5-year-olds – and Sweden, who in 2016 introduced the 'Teacher Salary Boost' initiative, aimed at improving the attractiveness of teaching as a profession (Litjens and Taguma, 2017[3]; Karlsson Lohmander, 2017[33]) (Box 2.1).

> **Box 2.1. Sweden's *Teacher Salary Boost* programme**
>
> In autumn 2016, Sweden introduced the "Teacher Salary Boost" (*Lönelyftet*) programme – a government-funded programme aimed at increasing the salaries of the most talented and highly skilled pre-primary and primary teachers. Under the scheme, certain teachers are selected for a salary increase of on average SEK 2 500–3 500 (EUR 230–330) per month. The municipality or the school or centre leaders decide how many and which teachers are qualified to receive a salary increase through the Teacher Salary Boost scheme, with guidance suggesting selection should based on staff skills and qualifications. Municipalities are also required to allocate resources within the school system according to the different conditions and needs of children (SFS 2016:100). The programme has the explicit goal of raising the recognition of the profession, in order to recruit more teachers, motivate new groups to become teachers, and encourage existing staff to stay in the profession. So far, the "Teacher Salary Boost" has provided 65 000 teachers with an average wage increase of SEK 2 600 (EUR 240) per month.
>
> In 2017, the Swedish Agency for Public Management published the first of three evaluations of the programme, with the final report expected in 2021. In the first early evaluation, the Agency considered take-up rates and management of the grants, and conducted interviews with school and centre leaders and participants. Findings suggest the programme benefited from very high take up, with as many as 90% of school authorities participating. Those who chose not to participate are mainly small independent education providers. They cited reasons related to maintaining cohesion and cooperation (over competition) in the workplace, uncertainty of long-term financing as well as of the full aspects of the regulation, related to the short notice given (Statskontoret, 2017[34]).
>
> The evaluation finds that grants were often given to the most skilled teachers, but were rarely allocated based on student needs, as required by the regulation. Only about 6% of administrators took student needs into account when allocating the increases (Statskontoret, 2017[34]). Furthermore, there was significant pessimism on the part of administrators around the benefits of the programme, mainly due to the limited scope and size of the government grant. For example, most principals believed the grant did not provide sufficient funds to reward all teachers they believed qualified (Statskontoret, 2017[34]). In all, the actual amount of the grant may not have offset the time and effort required to implement the policy. However, more time is needed to judge the full impact of the programme on job satisfaction and retention

2.2.3. Reducing barriers to entry

Careers in ECEC are relatively accessible compared to many other occupations, but some barriers remain. These mostly revolve around the pre-service training and qualification requirements present in many countries. Although pre-service training is important for process quality (Section 2.3) and professional status, it also has the potential to obstruct access for possible entrants without the resources to undergo formal training. High initial qualification requirements may deter or prevent some less academically minded workers from moving into the sector, for example. Similarly, absent of financial support, the costs of tuition and earnings foregone during training may discourage others. These issues are particularly relevant in the context of the low wages on offer in ECEC, since returns to pre-service training are likely to be lower than in other competing occupations.

Countries can help soften barriers to entry for new ECEC staff by funding and providing financial support through pre-service education and training. Japan, for example, provides funded pre-service training for day care staff with no previous experience, with the aim of increasing the attractiveness of the professional for new entrants (Litjens and Taguma, 2017[3]). In New Zealand, students training to become ECEC teachers can apply for 'TeachNZ' scholarships, covering the costs of tuition plus a grant of NZD 10 000 (EUR 6 000) (MoE, 2019[35]). In Denmark, pre-service ECEC training itself is free of charge, and students receive a 'practicum salary' from providers for some of the periods they are on practical placement (see Box 2.3). In 2017, this salary was worth about DKK 10 500 (EUR 1 400) per month. For the other placements as well as the time spent studying, they receive a student grant of roughly DKK 6 000 (EUR 800) per month from the government, and can take out a loan for up to roughly DKK 3 000 (EUR 400) per month (Oberhuemer and Schreyer, 2018[4]).

Countries can also promote access by providing alternative pathways for potential staff without pre-requisite qualifications. New Zealand, for instance, allows prospective workers who do not meet the entry criteria for an ECEC training programme to gain access through a bridging or foundation qualification. These programmes last up to one year, and prepare students for full pre-service training at university level. They also provide both educational institutions and students themselves with an indication of student capabilities, and help students with other commitments, such as family or work responsibilities, to determine whether further university-level training is a viable option (Litjens and Taguma, 2017[3]).

2.3. Improving pre-service training and 'job-readiness'

Pre-service education and training is crucial for the construction of a skilled and knowledgeable ECEC workforce. Although qualifications by themselves do not guarantee high quality teaching, studies from across the OECD demonstrate that better educated staff are generally better able to deliver high-quality early childhood education and care (OECD, 2012[1]; Wall, Litjens and Taguma, 2015[36]; OECD, 2018[2]). ECEC staff are expected to have specific skills, knowledge and competencies, and pre-service training helps new staff gains these skills. Highly qualified staff are better able to deliver a stimulating environment and provide high-quality interactions with children, leading to improvements in children's well-being, development, and learning outcomes (OECD, 2012[1]; OECD, 2001[37]; Wall, Litjens and Taguma, 2015[36]; OECD, 2018[2]). In addition, from a workforce perspective, thorough pre-service education and training helps reduce the risk that new staff struggle when entering the sector, potentially boosting retention.

Pre-service training requirements differ considerably across OECD countries. In many countries, staff in at least some roles are required to attain university-level qualifications before entering the sector (OECD, 2012[1]; EC/EACEA/Eurydice/Eurostat, 2014[38]). This is particularly common for centre leader or managers, and for those working in pre-primary education for older children, where the role is focused more on education and learning (see Table A.1). In France, Iceland, and Italy, pre-primary teachers are typically required to attain a master's level qualification. However, in a minority of countries (e.g. Austria, the Czech Republic, Germany, and the Slovak Republic) pre-primary teachers are required to hold only a post-secondary vocational qualification or below. Requirements are often (but not always) lower for staff in the care-oriented day care sector aimed at younger children (OECD, 2012[1]; EC/EACEA/Eurydice/Eurostat, 2014[38]).

Countries also differ in the degree of specialisation required during pre-service training. In most OECD countries, minimum qualification requirements refer to specific qualifications in ECEC. In others, they are broader. In France and the Netherlands, for example, pre-service training for pre-primary teachers is integrated with pre-service training for primary teachers. Graduates can work in either setting, and move between the two (Litjens and Taguma, 2017[3]; Oberhuemer and Schreyer, 2018[4]). This has the advantage of helping boost the pool of potential ECEC teachers, and could also contribute to increased status. However, it may not always to represent the best route to high-quality ECEC teaching: pre-primary teaching requires a different set of skills to primary teaching, and training in these specific skills is often delivered most effectively through specialised ECEC qualifications (OECD, 2018[2]).

Not all staff need to gain university-level qualifications before entering the sector (OECD, 2012[1]). Research indicates that highly qualified staff can have a positive influence on less-qualified colleagues working around them (OECD, 2012[1]; Sylva et al., 2010[39]), and for some staff, such as assistants and support staff, lower-level qualifications may be sufficient. Indeed, in several countries, there are currently no minimum qualification requirements for assistants and support staff (OECD, 2012[1]; EC/EACEA/Eurydice/Eurostat, 2014[38]). Furthermore, full-time university-level training also might not always be the most efficient or effective way of ensuring staff are 'job-ready'. In recent years, many countries have modified their pre-service training programmes towards a model that trains professionals 'on the job' inside of ECEC settings (Litjens and Taguma, 2017[3]).

2.3.1. Raising minimum qualification requirements

One of the most straightforward ways to boost the education levels of the ECEC workforce is to raise pre-service training and minimum qualification requirements. Qualification requirements guarantee that staff have a demonstrated level of knowledge and certain set of skills and competencies. Minimum qualification requirements should not be raised blindly and do not necessarily need to be uniform across all staff. Some roles in ECEC do not require a university-level qualification, for instance. However, where quality is a concern, raising qualification requirements for at least some staff (for example, for centre leaders) can help ensure that the workforce has the knowledge and skills to deliver high-quality ECEC.

Several OECD countries have raised or revised minimum qualification requirements in ECEC in recent decades, especially at the pre-primary level. Indeed, a clear trend has emerged in many countries for the alignment of pre-primary and primary teaching qualification requirements (OECD, 2017[32]). In the 1990s, Finland increased the minimum qualification requirement for pre-primary teachers to a university-level degree and aligned initial education more closely with primary teacher training, with a view to boosting quality and encourage co-operation between teachers during the transition from pre-primary to primary school (OECD, 2012[1]). In 1998, Portugal raised the minimum qualification requirement for pre-primary teachers from a three-year bachelor's degree to a four-year master's degree, setting initial education on par with teachers in primary and secondary education (OECD, 2012[1]). More recently, in 2009-10, Korea raised required pre-service training for pre-primary teachers to a four-year bachelor's degree, and also increased the length of upper-secondary level qualification required for staff in day-care centres (OECD, 2012[1]). In 2011, as one part of a wider reform of pre-service teacher training in general, Sweden introduced a requirement for all teaching staff to hold a three-and-a-half-year university degree (Eurydice, 2019[40]). Today, in 17 OECD countries, both pre-primary and primary teachers require a bachelor's level degree, and in a further six a master's degree is required at both levels (OECD, 2017[32]).

There are costs to increasing qualification requirements. Higher qualifications are likely to lead to demands for higher wages, increasing service costs. From a workforce perspective, there is also some risk that increasing minimum qualification requirements could intensify staff shortages. As touched on earlier, the costs and demands of formal training may deter or prevent some potential staff from entering the sector. In the short term, it also may be difficult to accommodate large numbers of new students within existing pre-service training institutions.

One approach in this situation is to moderate the requirement, typically by specifying that only a certain share of staff or only staff in certain roles (e.g. centre leaders) need to hold the required qualification. In England, for example, regulations stipulate that at least 50% of staff in charge of children under age 3 must have a relevant lower-secondary qualification, while at least one member of staff must have a qualification at upper-secondary level. For children over age 3, at least one staff member must have a higher vocational qualification corresponding to "Early Years Professional Status" (see Box 2.4), and another most hold an upper-secondary level qualification (Wall, Litjens and Taguma, 2015[36]).In Germany, some *Länder* (Bremen and Saxony) now stipulate that centre leaders in large centres must hold a relevant university-level qualification in ECEC, while remaining staff need only the standard vocational qualification at the post-secondary non-tertiary level (Lange, 2017[41]). In Norway, although not strictly a *requirement*, the most recent "*Strategy for Competence and Recruitment*" in ECEC places considerable emphasis on encouraging centre leaders to attain master's level education through in-service training (KD, 2017[42]).

A second option is to stagger the implementation of the new requirement. For example, in the mid-2000s, New Zealand initiated a process to increase the number of qualified and registered teachers in ECEC (see Box 2.2). Alongside other measures, they set out targets that required teacher-led ECEC services to have at least 50% or more of regulated staff that are registered teachers by 2007, increasing to 80% by 2010, and 100% by 2012. The ultimate 100% target has since been revised down to 80%, based on the view that eight out of ten is a sufficient ratio of qualified teachers. Nonetheless, together with other reforms, the introduction of the target led to a steady and sustained increase in the number of qualified and registered teachers in ECEC (Box 2.2).

Box 2.2. New Zealand's *Pathways to the Future* strategic plan for ECEC

In 2002, New Zealand introduced *Pathways to the Future: Ngā Huarahi Arataki*, a 10-year strategic plan describing strategies for the improvement of early childhood education services. A range of measures emerged from the plan, including policies to boost participation, to promote process quality, and to better support community-based services. Chief among these were two measures aimed at increasing the number of qualified and registered ECEC teachers.

First, the government set out targets that required teacher-led services to have at least 50% or more of regulated staff that are registered teachers by 2007 (which is still today the minimum requirement), with the aim of raising the target to 80% by 2010, and 100% by 2012. Second, to help compensate providers for the additional costs involved with employing greater numbers of registered staff, the government implemented a new system of supply-side public funding for ECEC. This new system was supported by a substantial increase in public ECEC spending.

Under the new funding system, public funds were to be allocated based largely on service cost. Public support would be distributed on a per-child basis, but with amounts differentiated by child age, by service type (teacher-led or parent-led, all-day or part-time), and by the number of staff who are qualified and registered ECEC teachers. Five 'quality funding bands' were introduced, linked to the share of staff (0–29%, 25–49%, 50–79%, 80–99%, and 100%) registered with, and holding a qualification approved by, the New Zealand Teachers' Council. The aim was to deliver higher funding to providers with higher shares of registered teachers, helping them meet the increased wage costs associated with qualified and registered teachers (Mitchell et al., 2011[43]).

In 2010, the 100% target was reduced to 80% by the government, based on the consideration that eight out of ten is a sufficient ratio of qualified teachers. The funding for centres that had reached 100% of qualified teachers was aligned with the level of funding for centres with at least 80%. At the same time, the subsidy for these centres was reduced due to budget constraints (Meade et al., 2012[44]).

Despite the partial cutbacks, available evidence suggests that, together with other initiatives, the registered teacher target and new funding system were successful in promoting the number of qualified staff in ECEC. Between 2004 and 2005, the share of qualified and registered teachers in teacher-led ECEC services jumped by 15 percentage points, from 37% to 52% (MoE, 2008[45]). By 2013, it had climbed to 75% (MoE, 2019[46]).[4] As many as 94% of teacher-led centre-based services had 80% or more qualified and registered teachers (MoE, 2013[47]). The Teacher's Work Study by the New Zealand Childcare Association compared the teaching and learning in education and care centres which had 50-79% qualified teachers to centres with 100% qualified staff. It found that children in the latter centres benefitted from the higher qualification of staff as the greater pedagogical experience of these centres' teachers helped children's cognitive development, e.g. by fostering more complex play and sustained shared thinking (Meade et al., 2012[44]).

2.3.2. Including practical experience in pre-service training

Pre-service training in ECEC requires a mixture of theory and practice. While classroom-based learning on the theory of ECEC is important, trainee ECEC workers also need real-world experience and the opportunity to apply their knowledge in a practical setting. Practical experience provides new staff with an opportunity to familiarise themselves with the dynamics of teaching in context and helps lessen the need for an adjustment period when first entering employment. Evidence from primary and secondary education suggests that students with more field experience have higher retention levels than those who do not (Litjens and Taguma, 2017[3]).

Many OECD countries already include practical experience and workplace-based learning in their pre-service training programmes (Litjens and Taguma, 2017[3]; OECD, 2017[32]). Modern training programmes combine extensive coursework and classroom-based learning on how to teach with an extended period gathering practical experience inside ECEC settings. During this time, students are able to familiarise themselves with the ECEC environment, put acquired knowledge into practice, and to develop their own strategies and innovative practices.

Several OECD countries provide good examples of integrating practical experience into pre-service training (Litjens and Taguma, 2017[3]). Denmark provides one of the most comprehensive examples – there, student ECEC teachers must complete the equivalent of more than one year of practical placements (Box 2.3). Other examples include Norway, where student ECEC teachers are required to complete at least 100 days practical placement (Litjens and Taguma, 2017[3]); Italy, where the master's level pre-primary teacher training programme includes 600 hours of compulsory placement (Oberhuemer and Schreyer, 2018[4]); Germany, where details of the post-secondary level pre-service ECEC teacher training programme vary across *Länder* but often include one-year of practical placement (Oberhuemer and Schreyer, 2018[4]); and Sweden, where students training to become ECEC teachers complete 20-weeks' worth of practical placements (Oberhuemer and Schreyer, 2018[4]).

Box 2.3. Practical placements in Denmark's initial ECEC teacher training programme

In Denmark, the pre-service training programme for ECEC teachers places considerable emphasis on practical experience and classroom-based learning. To become an ECEC teacher, students must complete a three-and-a-half-year bachelor's degree, a third of which consists of practical placements inside of ECEC settings (Oberhuemer and Schreyer, 2018[4]). The aim is not just to help students gain experience, but also to acquire knowledge (Litjens and Taguma, 2017[3]).

The practical placements take place in four blocks. The first lasts for 32 days with students working an average of six hours per day. The second and third last for six months at an average of 32.5 hours per week. The fourth lasts for only 16 days. During the first and second placement, the provider and a supervisor from the student's university evaluate performance internally. During the third, an external examiner is also present. During the fourth, students collect empirical data for their end of study thesis. Students receive payment throughout. For the first and fourth placements, student receive a state-funded student grant. During the second and third, students are paid by the provider (Litjens and Taguma, 2017[3]; Oberhuemer and Schreyer, 2018[4]).

A qualified ECEC teacher supervises students throughout their placements. Supervision and guidance is provided both informally throughout the day, and more formally through planned meetings. Estimates suggest that these meetings last for an average of one hour per week. Placement supervisors receive a small wage bonus for the role. In 2014, the bonus was about EUR 550 for a six-month placement (Oberhuemer and Schreyer, 2018[4]).

2.3.3. Providing alternative pathways into the sector

In most OECD countries, specialised pre-service training is lengthy. This is especially the case at the pre-primary level, where pre-service training often lasts for three, four or even five years (OECD, 2014[24]). These courses are key for preparing future ECEC workers. However, their duration, together at times with their entry requirements, places limits on the number of potential workers that can apply. For example, many younger workers may be hesitant about continuing in full-time education and keen instead to get straight into work. Graduates who have already completed a university degree in an unrelated discipline may be reluctant to return for a second three-year-plus course. Older workers, many of whom may have acquired relevant skills from working in other occupations, are likely to be similarly unenthusiastic about committing to a lengthy university-level qualification. The result is that restrictive pre-service training requirements may prevent skilled and talented workers from entering the industry.

Countries can widen the pool of potential workers by providing alternative educational pathways into the sector. One option is to offer apprenticeships, whereby trainees combine work with practical on the job training and study. This is likely to be particularly attractive to younger workers without the qualifications needed to enter full pre-service training programmes. England, for example, provides a range of ECEC apprenticeship programmes to unqualified entrants that end in qualifications at lower- or upper-secondary level (National Apprenticeship Service, 2018[48]). Exact details vary between providers and across levels, but the apprenticeships usually last between one and two years, during which time apprentices work under the supervision of qualified staff and are afforded one day per week to study (National Apprenticeship Service, 2018[49]; Oberhuemer and Schreyer, 2018[4]). Apprenticeships are also common in Finland. This is especially the case for entrants looking to train for the three-year upper-secondary level "Children's instructor" (*Lastenohjaaja*) qualification, after which they are qualified to work in a support 'co-worker' role (Oberhuemer and Schreyer, 2018[4]). More recently, some German *Länder* (Baden-Württemberg, Bavaria, Hesse and North Rhine-Westphalia) have begun to provide apprenticeship-style entry routes for ECEC teacher qualifications, with students combining theoretical studies with paid work in an ECEC setting (Oberhuemer and Schreyer, 2018[4]). In one *Land* to offer this option (Baden-Württemberg), students receive a monthly wage of EUR 1 600 while they complete their qualification (Oberhuemer and Schreyer, 2018[4]).

Older workers likely require a different approach. One option is to implement programmes that recognise and validate skills and competencies gained outside of ECEC. In Finland, for instance, staff looking to work in certain support roles have the option of gaining the required upper-secondary level qualification through a demonstration, either partially or fully, of the relevant vocational skills (Oberhuemer and Schreyer, 2018[4]). The resulting qualification is fully equivalent to that gained through the conventional training course.

A second is to offer accelerated programmes to prospective staff with relevant experience or relevant but not directly applicable qualifications. Sweden, for instance, recently introduced 14 'fast-track' programmes for newly arrived immigrants with education, training or work experience in areas for which there is demand in Sweden, including one for pre-primary and primary teachers with a migrant background and a teaching qualification from another country (Oberhuemer and Schreyer, 2018[4]; Lärarförbundet, 2018[50]). The programme offers quicker progression and a faster pathway to qualified teacher status than the standard route. It can be completed in just one year (compared to the three-and-a-half-year standard qualification), and includes training in the Swedish education system, plus work experience (Lärarförbundet, 2018[50]). Given the large number of migrants that have recently entered Sweden, it is hoped that the programme may go some way towards addressing existing staff shortages (Oberhuemer and Schreyer, 2018[4]).

A third option is to provide similarly accelerated programmes to potential staff with unrelated but valued backgrounds and experience. As just one example, in England between 2007 and 2014, university graduates from any discipline had the opportunity to attain what was known as *Early Years Professional Status* (EYPS) (Box 2.4). Motivated by studies that found process quality was higher in centres led by university graduates, EYPS was awarded to ECEC workers with university-level qualifications following a period of placement, training and assessment, or alternatively to university graduates not working in the sector through a one-year training programme. Among other objectives, the goal was to make better use of the many university graduates keen and available to work in the sector without requiring them to go through lengthy pre-service training. The programme was largely successful in this aim – in the five years following the introduction of the EYPS award, the share of graduates in private full-day care centres more than doubled. However, it has since been replaced by a successor award, *Early Years Teacher Status (EYTS)*. More so than the former EYPS award, EYTS places strong emphasis on training candidates as specialists in early childhood development and education, and is intended to match the standards set for primary and secondary education teachers (Box 2.4).

Box 2.4. England's Early Years Professional Programme

In 2007, England introduced its *Early Years Professional Programme* (EYPP), a series of measures aimed at bringing university-educated staff into the dominant private, voluntary and independent (PVI) ECEC sector. Motivated by studies that found university graduate-led centres provide higher quality services (Sylva et al., 2010[51]), the aim at the time was to require all day care centres to have at least one university-educated member of staff with accredited "Early Years Professional Status" by 2015. *Early Years Professional Status* (EYPS) was not a qualification in its own right. Rather, it was an award given to staff with university-level qualifications (in any discipline) following a period of placement, training and assessment. University graduates not already working in the sector could also attain EYPS through an alternative one-year training programme.

The EYPP had several objectives. As well as improving process quality, it was hoped that the introduction of the EYPS award would help contribute to the professionalisation of the sector, improve options for career progression, help challenge early years practitioners' perceived lack of status, and encourage graduates to join the ECEC workforce. It was also hoped that workers with EYPS would also use their skills to improve practice and help other workers develop.

By many measures, the EYPP was successful in achieving several of its aims. Following the introduction of the EYPP, the share of staff in private full-day care centres with at least a university degree more than doubled, from 5% in 2008 to 13% in 2013 (Brind et al., 2014[52]). The share of senior managers with a degree also almost doubled, from 17% in 2008 to 33% in 2013 (Brind et al., 2014[52]). A Department of Education-commissioned evaluation of the programme by the University of Wolverhampton concluded that the EYPP had "a very positive impact … in supporting workforce development" and that it helped create "a cohort of workers that are more willing and confident to take on leadership roles and enact improvements to service delivery" (Hadfield et al., 2012[53]). It also found that attaining EYPS has helped many staff improve their own sense of status. A second study focusing on process quality found that gaining a member of staff with EYPS was associated with a significant improvement in quality (Mathers et al., 2011[54]).

However, although successful in several ways, there remained concerns around the status of the EYPS award, as well as the level and rigour of pre-service training involved when gaining EYPS (Nutbrown, 2012[55]). These revolved in particular around the lack of parity between EYPS and the qualifications held by teachers in the primary and secondary education sectors. In 2012, the government-commissioned *Nutbrown Review of Early Education and Childcare Qualifications* (Nutbrown, 2012[55]) recommended that the EYPS award be replaced by a new early years teacher qualification that would provide greater teaching-oriented training and match the rigour and status of primary and secondary education teaching qualifications.

> In 2014, the *Early Years Professional Programme* was superseded by the *Early Years Teacher Programme* (EYTP). In line with the Nutbrown recommendation, the new programme abandoned the EYPS award and replaced it with the *Early Years Teacher Status* (EYTS) qualification, which places greater emphasis on teaching-oriented education and training. Students studying for the EYTS qualification train as specialists in early childhood education and development. The qualification is intended to be equivalent to those for teachers in primary and secondary education, although it does not carry an entitlement to the same pay or conditions. It is too soon for a full evaluation of the EYTP. However, figures from the *Childcare and Early Years Providers Survey 2018* suggest that growth in the number of graduates working in ECEC has slowed since its introduction. In 2018, 13% of staff in full-day care centres had a university degree – the same as in 2013 (DfE, 2018[56]).

2.4. Bringing men into the ECEC workforce

Several countries in the OECD are attempting to diversify the ECEC workforce by increasing the numbers of male staff. Bringing men into ECEC jobs is increasingly recognised as having the potential to improve process quality and child development and learning, particularly in the development of attitudes towards gender roles (Litjens and Taguma, 2017[3]; Sumsion, 2005[57]; Peeters, 2007[58]). Men are now seen as important to children's development, and research shows that male workers are well-received by female colleagues (Peeters, Rohrmann and Emilsen, 2015[59]).

In the late 1990s, a network of ECEC experts convened by the European Commission set a 20% minimum target for the share of ECEC staff that should be male. Countries like Belgium, Denmark, Germany, Norway, and the United Kingdom have developed policies or programmes to address this issue (Oberhuemer, 2011[60]), but achieving gender balance in early childhood education remains a challenge across the OECD.

Despite the benefits of increasing the male ECEC workforce, the number of men in pre-primary and childcare positions remains very low. On average in the OECD, just 3.2% of pre-primary teachers are male. The rate is lower than 1% in most of Eastern Europe, Israel, and Portugal (Figure 2.4). Top performers are the Netherlands, France, and Norway, where 7.5 to 12.5% of pre-primary teachers are men. Gender balance in the care-oriented sector aimed at younger children is equally poor (OECD, 2018[19]). As the pre-school years are an age where conceptions of gender roles and stereotypes are often formed (Martin and Ruble, 2004[61]; Martin and Ruble, 2010[62]), this gender imbalance in teaching and caregiving does not bode well for gender norms in the future.

Figure 2.4. Few men hold ECEC jobs

Distribution of pre-primary education teachers by sex, all ages, 2016

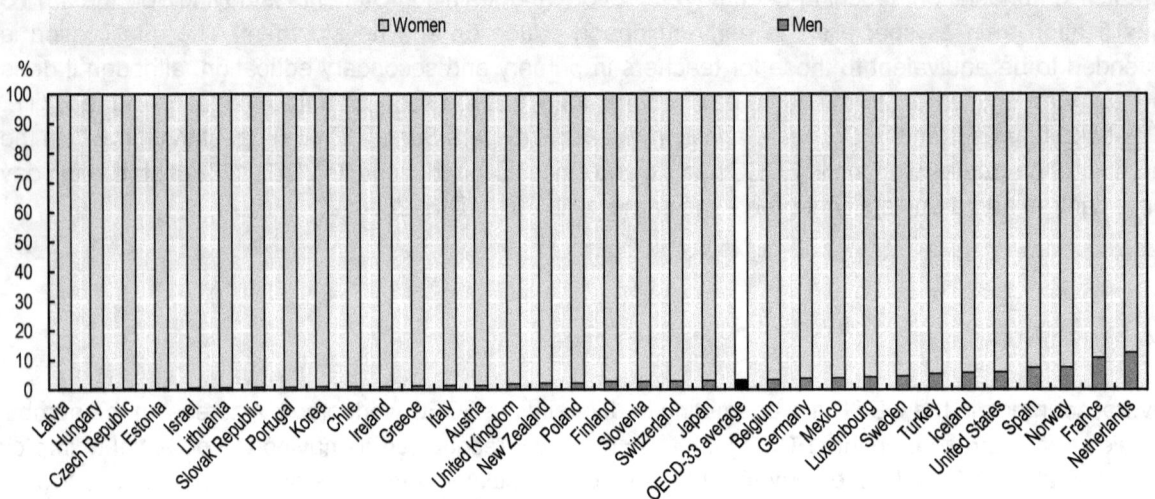

Note: 'Pre-primary education teachers' refers to teachers in pre-primary education (ISCED2011 level 0 programme 2). Data for Italy refer to 2012, for Estonia to 2014, and for New Zealand to 2015.
Source: OECD Education Database, http://www.oecd.org/education/database.htm.

In many OECD countries, the absolute number of men in caregiving has risen dramatically over the past two decades. But as jobs in the ECEC sector have also grown rapidly, the increasing numbers of men are not necessarily reflected in higher male: female ratios (Peeters, Rohrmann and Emilsen, 2015[59]). In Turkey, for example, the number of men working in ECEC nearly quintupled in ten years, from 694 men in 2003-04 to 3 387 in 2013 to 2014, but since childcare supply grew simultaneously, men in Turkey still only make up about 5% of ECEC workers (Peeters, Rohrmann and Emilsen, 2015[59]). This illustrates the importance of promoting gender balance in staffing expansions of childcare and preschool provision.

Preferences and attitudes towards ECEC careers are formed early. Results from the OECD Programme of International Student Assessment (PISA) show that female 15-year-old students are, on average, 16 times more likely than male 15-year-old students to report that they want to work as preschool teachers or childcare providers in their future career (Figure 2.5). On average in the OECD, only 0.2% of boys say they expect to work in ECEC at age 30, compared to 3.2% of girls.

Figure 2.5. Boys are far less likely than girls to expect a career in ECEC

Percentage of 15-year-old students who expect to work in early childhood education and care when they are age 30, by sex, 2015

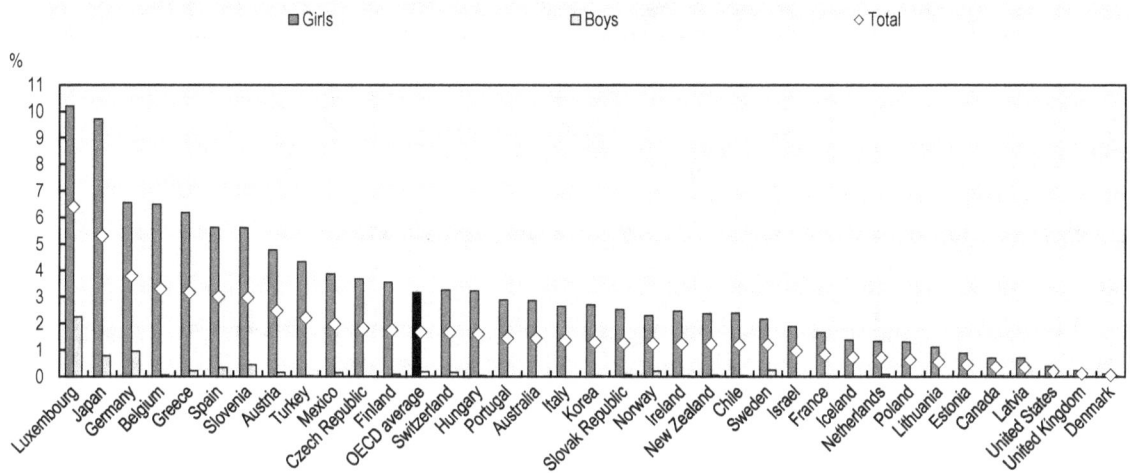

Note: 15-year-old students were asked "What kind of job do you expect to have when you are about 30 years old?" Answers to the question were coded using the ISCO-08 (International Standard of Classification of Occupations) classification of occupations at the 4-digit level. Students who "expect to work in early childhood education and care" are those with answers coded under ISCO-08 groups 2342 ("Early childhood educators") or 5311 ("Child care workers"). On average across OECD countries, an additional 0.15% gave answers that were coded under the broader ISCO-08 groups 234 ("Primary school and early childhood teachers") or 531 ("Child care workers and teachers' aides") but could not be further defined. These students are not included in the figure. The difference between boys and girls is statistically significant at p<0.05 in all countries shown other than Denmark.
Source: OECD calculations based on the OECD Programme for International Student Assessment (PISA) 2015 Database, http://www.oecd.org/pisa/.

Many reasons explain the dearth of men in ECEC jobs. The professions' often low social status is one factor, as is low pay (Section 2.2). Yet better salaries and higher social status are unlikely to be sufficient to close the gender gap. It is important to improve recruitment, foster networks for male ECEC workers, and – crucially – change gendered perceptions of certain occupations (OECD, 2017[63]), as the perceived attractiveness of child caregiving jobs is formed early in life (Figure 2.5 above). In some countries, like Norway, affirmative action has also played a role in getting more men into ECEC jobs.

2.4.1. Using campaigns to attract male workers

An important first step in improving gender diversity in the ECEC workforce is fostering public support for men in teaching and caring for young children, both in terms of improving norms around men as caregivers and in recruiting male workers. Information campaigns among students, potential (male) applicants, hiring managers, and parents are important for opening up this field.

Some governments are getting involved to address the imbalance. In Scotland, for example, the government in 2018 introduced a new GBP 50 000 fund for pilot projects aimed at getting more men into ECEC. Scotland also supports the non-profit "Men in Childcare" foundation, which subsidises certified courses necessary for a career in early years care.

Denmark and Belgium have used marketing campaigns to foster the public image of male childcare workers. In the Flemish Community of Belgium, a poster campaign was the chief media tool. The poster was picked up by media channels, which helped with dissemination. The Belgian campaign also created recruitment guidelines and an event. By the end of the one-year campaign, there was a slight increase in the share of students at a training centre for childcare who were male, and most of the students indicated that the campaign influenced them in enrolling in the course (Litjens and Taguma, 2017[3]).

In Denmark, which has one of the world's highest rates of ECEC workers who are male, the former Ministry of Children, Education and Gender Equality carried out a recruitment initiative for men in five local municipalities. The results of this campaign were reported in a handbook for other municipalities (Jensen, 2017[64]). And in 2016, the Ministry launched a campaign which included a widely-shared Facebook video and free conferences at several universities on the theme "More Men in ECEC" (Jensen, 2017[64]).

Information and public awareness campaigns are rarely rigorously analysed, but any such efforts could be studied – with adequate pre-planning – with an experimental design.

2.4.2. Improving male worker support and networking initiatives

Networking and peer-to-peer support are also important for promoting gender diversity in so-called "one-gender" jobs. Networking, peer support and mentorship programmes are commonly used to help women to enter, remain in, and advance in domains that are traditionally male-dominated, such as the STEM fields and entrepreneurship (OECD, 2017[63]). While it is difficult to quantify the benefit of such programmes, they likely exert a positive effect on attractive and retaining a diverse workforce.

In the United Kingdom, several local or non-profit initiatives are underway, but there has not been a serious national government-organised effort. The "Men in the Early Years" (MITEY) campaign, run by a civil society group, has held conferences annually since 2015. It runs events and publishes materialises aimed at raising awareness of the need for more men working with children, providing managers in the ECEC sector with resources to help in recruiting men, and promoting child caregiving careers to men. Some local governments are prioritising this issue, too; in Bristol, for example, "the Bristol Men in Early Years Network" serves as a network of educators encouraging gender equality in the early years sector (www.bmiey.co.uk). Rigorous empirical analyses of the results of these and similar networks are lacking.

2.4.3. Implementing affirmative action policies favouring male candidates

Affirmative action in hiring – the practice of favouring individuals belonging to groups known to have been discriminated against previously – has been infrequently used to get more men into ECEC jobs. One exception is Norway (Box 2.5). These types of measures have been helpful in other sectors in improving gender equality, e.g. for improving the share of public leaders or corporate board members who are women (OECD, 2017[63]). Affirmative action measures should ideally serve as a temporary transition to long-term changes in systems and cultures whereby women and men contribute on an equal footing.

Box 2.5. Affirmative action to get men in ECEC in Norway

Norway has made sustained efforts to improve the gender balance of the ECEC workforce over the past three decades. As far back as 1990, the Norwegian government introduced a range of measures aimed at encouraging men to enter the sector, including the development of networks for male workers, conferences on the issue, and the preparation of documents and videos to stimulate discussion (OECD, 2001[37]). In 1997, it launched the first of a series of action plans to bring men into ECEC including, among other measures, a goal of men making up at least 20% of the ECEC workforce by 2000. In 1998, the government agreed that positive action could be applied to the recruitment of men into ECEC jobs – the first time that positive action had been applied to men (OECD, 2001[37]). More recently, regulations have been introduced to promote male recruitment, including an affirmative action policy favouring a male candidate if two applicants have same qualifications (Engel et al., 2015[9]).

While Norway has not yet met its own target for a 20% male workforce, its measures have contributed to a steady increase in the male share of ECEC workers. Statistics Norway reports that male employees in ECEC rose from 9.9% of the total kindergarten workforce in 2015 to 10.1% in 2016 and 10.3% in 2017 (SSB, 2019[65]). Norway also reports that the proportion of male students registering for kindergarten teacher education has increased in recent years, though the dropout rate is still higher for men than for women (Engel et al., 2015[9]).

3 Retaining and developing highly-skilled staff

Policies to attract and recruit ECEC staff need to be matched by strategies to keep skilled staff inside the sector. Given the size of the early childcare sector, even small changes in the rate of staff retention could have large repercussions on the demand for new staff and how much is asked of remaining staff (Litjens and Taguma, 2017[3]). If ECEC systems are to ensure a quality workforce, they not only need to bring talented people into the sector, but also retain skilled workers and further develop the professionals currently employed.

Retaining skilled staff is important not just for economic reasons. The early childhood literature points to a stable relationship with a caring adult as a key component of a child's development. Secure and trusted relationships affect language and vocabulary skills in addition to emotional stability (Bridges et al., 2011[66]; Wells, 2015[67]; Hale-Jinks, Knopf and Knopf, 2006[68]). High staff turnover in ECEC can be disruptive, forcing children to re-form relationships and, as a result, spend less time taking part in meaningful activities (OECD, 2012[1]).

A number of factors influence ECEC staff retention. Wages are one of the most frequently cited predictors of turnover, but others include working conditions, job satisfaction, and opportunities for development and progression. Totenhagen, et al. (2016[18]) conduct a review of the empirical literature on retaining ECEC workers and find seven themes for predicting retention: wages and benefits, job satisfaction, organisational characteristics, alternative employment opportunities, demographic and job characteristics, as well as education and training. These factors can combine, reinforce, and amplify one another. One study (Wells, 2015[69]) found that it is the accumulation of "risk factors" (including low pay and recognition, low job satisfaction, and a difficult relationship with the supervisor) that greatly increase the chances of quitting. In general, research indicates that improvements in areas such as child-to-staff ratios, wages and benefits, schedule and workload, and the physical and emotional environment can lead to improvements in job satisfaction and retention (OECD, 2012[1]).

This section covers policies and strategies for retaining and developing ECEC staff. It starts with a discussion of the importance of improving pay and recognition and the effects of efforts to boost wages on staff retention. The second sub-section looks at policies and initiatives to improve working conditions, with particular attention paid to strategies to improve regulatory standards, including child-to-staff ratios. The third and final sub-section discusses measures to promote in-service training and professional development opportunities, and especially strategies to encourage staff to engage in training and development.

3.1. Main findings

- Strategies to keep skilled staff inside the ECEC sector are crucial for the construction of a high-quality ECEC workforce. Low pay is one factor often cited by workers considering leaving the sector, and efforts to boost wages in general are likely to help improve staff retention. In addition, however, countries should consider revising wage structures and/or engaging in measures that reward performance and development through improved pay.

- Countries should also engage in strategies to enhance working conditions. Improving regulatory standards, including by reducing minimum child-to-staff ratios, is one option open to countries, even though such a move is likely to place an additional burden on public budgets. Smaller class sizes are important for service quality and can help improve worker retention by, for instance, reducing stress among staff.
- Countries should also consider engaging in activities to promote in-service training and professional development opportunities. This is vital for process quality, and may help boost sector-wide retention by, for example, enhancing professional identity and improving career satisfaction. Importantly, just providing the option of training is not enough; countries should also use strategies to promote and encourage staff participation. Mandating in-service training is one option. Introducing measures that incentivise training is another.

3.2. Improving pay and recognition

Unsurprisingly, low wages are a major reason frequently cited by ECEC staff considering leaving a job or even the sector altogether (Totenhagen et al., 2016[18]; Irvine et al., 2016[15]). As outlined in Section 2.2, wages in ECEC are generally very low, especially in the care-oriented day care sector aimed at very young children. These low wages damage retention. One study from the United States found that only 25% of staff in the lowest wage category had worked in their current centre for at least five years, compared to 90% of workers in the highest wage category. This difference translates to a 6% decrease in the likelihood that an ECEC worker will have left the centre for every one U.S. dollar increase in the hourly wage (Totenhagen et al., 2016[18]).

Low wages and a lack of recognition present a significant challenge for staff retention. Many ECEC workers have opportunities to work elsewhere for higher pay, which leaves providers reliant on the intrinsic motivation of its workers for retention. Yet, vocational commitment and the "love of children" is not able to overcome low wages if staff do not have alternative sources of household income, nor is educators' household income an appropriate subsidy for the provision of early childcare education (Irvine et al., 2016[15]). This further contributes to the perception that the ECEC sector is a low-status profession, or the stigma that "we're just babysitters," as described by one child care director from Brisbane, Australia (McDonald, Thorpe and Irvine, 2018[14]).

Many OECD countries are attempting to raise wages in ECEC. As discussed earlier in Section 2.2.2, several countries (the Czech Republic, Hungary, Korea, Portugal, New Zealand and the Slovak Republic) have recently introduced pay parity between pre-primary and primary teachers (Litjens and Taguma, 2017[3]; OECD, 2017[32]). These measures, as well as others like New Zealand's cost-based system of supply-side funding (Box 2.2), are important for staff retention as well as recruitment.

Countries can also help boost retention through wage structures and initiatives that reward performance and development. In the pre-primary sector at least, teachers typically receive salary increases throughout their careers based on experience, grade and/or qualification level (Litjens and Taguma, 2017[3]). On average across OECD countries, the annual salary of a public-sector pre-primary teacher with 15 years' experience is roughly 34% higher than the statutory starting salary (Figure 3.1). However, tenure-based wage increases do not necessarily reward performance and may inadvertently advantage weaker staff with fewer employment opportunities elsewhere. Explicitly tying wages to performance is difficult in sectors like ECEC where there are few easily measurable performance indicators. Instead, one option is to link pay increases to staff training and professional development activities. Two examples from the United

States demonstrate how providing wage boosts and salary supplements based on education and professional development can help reduce turnover and boost retention (Box 3.1).

Figure 3.1. Salary progression for pre-primary teachers varies across OECD countries

Annual statutory teachers' salaries in public pre-primary institutions over the course of the career, USD PPP, 2017

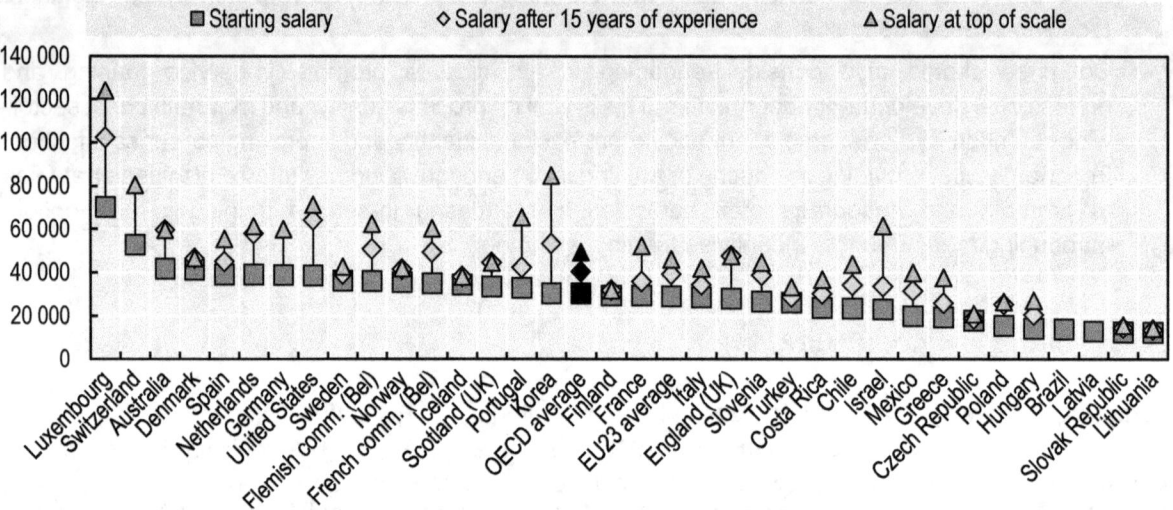

Note: Statutory salaries based on pay scales and the most prevalent qualifications in public institutions at each stage of the career. Statutory salaries are only one component of teachers' total compensation. Education systems also offer additional payments to teachers, such as allowances, bonuses or other rewards. For Finland, data on pre-primary teachers includes the salary of kindergarten teachers, who are the majority. For Germany, statutory salaries vary considerably depending on collective bargaining agreement. The data shown refer to gross basic starting salary and highest possible gross basic salary for a pre-primary teacher ("Erzieher") 'with demanding tasks' covered by the TVöD SuE collective agreement for workers in public social and educational services.
Source: OECD (2018), *OECD Education at a Glance 2018*, http://www.oecd.org/education/education-at-a-glance/; for Germany, OECD calculations based on information from Oberhuemer and Schreye (2018[4]).

Box 3.1. The *Child Care WAGE$ Initiative* and *Workforce Incentive Project* in the United States

Child Care WAGE$ Initiative in North Carolina (United States)

The Child Care WAGE$ initiative in North Carolina (United States) is an education-based salary supplement for ECEC workers aimed at increasing the attractiveness of ECEC as a profession for educated teachers. As part of the programme, participants receive a financial reward issued bi-annually, upon completion of six months in the same ECEC centre. The programme is implemented by a local non-profit organization under the supervision of the North Carolina state government. In 2017-18, the average six-month supplement was USD 902 (equivalent to an annual salary increase of about EUR 1 600) (T.E.A.C.H Early Childhood National Center, 2017[70]).

Evaluations suggest the WAGE$ initiative has helped improve retention. Turnover rates for participants in WAGE$ over the last decade range from 12% to 18%, significantly below its stated goal of 25% and industry national averages of around 30% to 40% (T.E.A.C.H Early Childhood National Center, 2017[70]). A large majority of participants (96%) report believing that the salary supplements either encouraged them to stay in their current settings or to pursue further education, with 97% of them reporting feeling less stressed, more appreciated, and better recognised due to the programme (T.E.A.C.H Early Childhood National Center, 2017[70]). Furthermore, education levels also increased among WAGE$

participants. In 2017, 74% of WAGE$ participants had an Associate's degree in early childhood education, compared to only 30% of active participants in 1999, its first year of state-wide implementation (T.E.A.C.H Early Childhood National Center, 2017[70]).

Workforce Incentive Project (W.I.N.) in Missouri (United States)

The Workforce Incentive Project (W.I.N.) in Missouri is a public and privately funded programme that issues bi-annual wage supplements to ECEC staff based on educational attainment. The programme has a primary goal to reduce ECEC staff turnover, and a secondary objective of encouraging staff to engage in education, training, and professional development (Gable et al., 2007[71]). Eligibility for the programme depends on qualifications and tenure: all staff with at least upper-secondary education and a service record of at least 30 hours per week for at least nine months per year are eligible. The programme deliberately includes staff with an upper-secondary qualification but without any further formal post-secondary education, as a key aim is to encourage less educated staff to pursuit further studies. The annual wage supplements delivered to participants range from USD 500 (about EUR 450) for a staff member with upper-secondary education to USD 2 500 (EUR 2 200) for a staff member with a specific Master's-level qualification in ECEC or child development (Gable et al., 2007[71]).

Evaluations suggest the programme is likely to have helped improve staff retention. Based on a quasi-experimental design and survival analysis, Gabel et al. (2007[71]) find that W.I.N. participation is associated with lower rates of turnover in teaching staff, even after controlling for other factors such as job satisfaction, location (urban, suburban or rural) and hourly wage, though no such association was found for centre managers. Notably, Gabel et al. (2007[71]) find that the positive effect on teaching staff retention is stronger for staff with above-median levels of education, experience, and hourly wages. The authors interpret this finding as suggesting that cash incentives could serve as a welcome bonus for more highly qualified or experienced staff, decreasing their probability to seek out higher paying jobs (Gable et al., 2007[71]).

3.3. Improving working conditions

Wages are not the only factor driving low retention. ECEC staff considering leaving their jobs also often point to stress, burnout and poor support as key reasons (Totenhagen et al., 2016[18]). Several studies show that workers reporting emotional exhaustion and/or poor working conditions are more likely than others to express an intention to leave (Manlove and Guzell, 1997[72]; Grant, Jeon and Buettner, 2019[73]). For example, one study from the United States found that a one-unit increase in emotional exhaustion (measured as low, medium, or high) doubled the likelihood of an individual leaving their job (Manlove and Guzell, 1997[72]). Another found that feeling poorly supported at work is a far stronger predictor of intention to leave than the actual work itself (Wells, 2015[69]). Workload is also correlated with quality, in that staff with heavier workloads tend to perform worse than those with lighter schedules (OECD, 2012[1]; Grant, Jeon and Buettner, 2019[73]). Improving working conditions and staff support structures can help increase staff performance, boost job satisfaction, improve staff-child interactions, and reduce turnover (OECD, 2012[1]; Ackerman, 2006[16]; Schreyer and Krause, 2016[74]; Totenhagen et al., 2016[18]; OECD, 2018[2]).

By several measures, working conditions in ECEC are poorer than those in competing occupations, such as primary education. For example, although total working time is often similar in pre-primary and primary education, there are typically major differences in the structure of working time and in how staff spend their time at work (OECD, 2017[32]). In many OECD countries, pre-primary teachers spend more time than primary teachers in direct contact with children (Figure 3.2, Panel A), and less on other duties (Figure 3.2, Panel B). Indeed, on average across OECD countries with available data, total annual direct contact time for teachers in public pre-primary education institutions is 260 hours longer than direct contact time for primary education teachers. As a result, pre-primary teachers often have less paid time for activities such as preparation and meetings with colleagues and parents, with the risk being that they end up making up the difference through unpaid work in their free time.

Working conditions can be influenced through the setting of minimum regulatory standards, such as those governing the number of children per staff member and the space for a given number of children (Litjens and Taguma, 2017[3]). Child-to-staff ratios are perhaps the most frequently cited and heavily monitored minimum standard. Lower child-to-staff ratios provide more opportunities for interaction between staff and children, and lead to interactions that are more meaningful (OECD, 2012[1]). And in addition to the direct effect on process quality, child-to-staff ratios also impact the working environment. When asked through questionnaires and interviews, staff report feeling more supported and less stress when responsible for a smaller group of children, and that staff-child dialogue and other activities suffer when group size increases (Pramling-Samuelsson et al., 2016[75]).

Currently, child-to-staff ratios in pre-primary education services differ considerably across OECD countries (Figure 3.3). In 2016, the average child-to-*teaching*-staff ratio across OECD countries was 14.2 – meaning that there was approximately 14 children for every teacher in pre-primary education – but this varied from more than 20 children per teacher in Chile, France and Mexico to fewer than ten in Germany, Iceland, Latvia, and Slovenia. However, some OECD countries make extensive use of teacher's assistants at the pre-primary level. As a result, in several countries, the child-to-*contact*-staff ratio is considerably lower than the child-to-teaching-staff ratio (Figure 3.3). Child-to-staff ratios are generally a little lower in services aimed at younger children. In Iceland, for example, the child-to-teaching staff ratio for early childhood educational development services in 2016 was as low as 3.2, meaning there are approximately three children per member of teaching staff.

Several OECD countries have introduced measures to improve ECEC child-to-staff ratios and strengthen regulatory standards more generally. For example, in 2005, Korea tightened regulations to improve standards in day care centres. The maximum staff-to-child ratio was reduced from five to three for children under age one, and set at five for 1-year-olds; seven for 2-year-olds; 15-20 for 3-year-olds; and 20 for 4-and 5-year-olds (Litjens and Taguma, 2017[3]). Other measures included regulations on the maximum number of children per centre (300) and on regulated floor space per child (raised from 3.64 to 4.29 square metres per child) (Litjens and Taguma, 2017[3]).

Figure 3.2. Most pre-primary teachers in the OECD spend more hours in direct contact with children than primary teachers

Net teaching time and time spent on other duties over the school year, public pre-primary and primary education institutions, hours per year, 2017

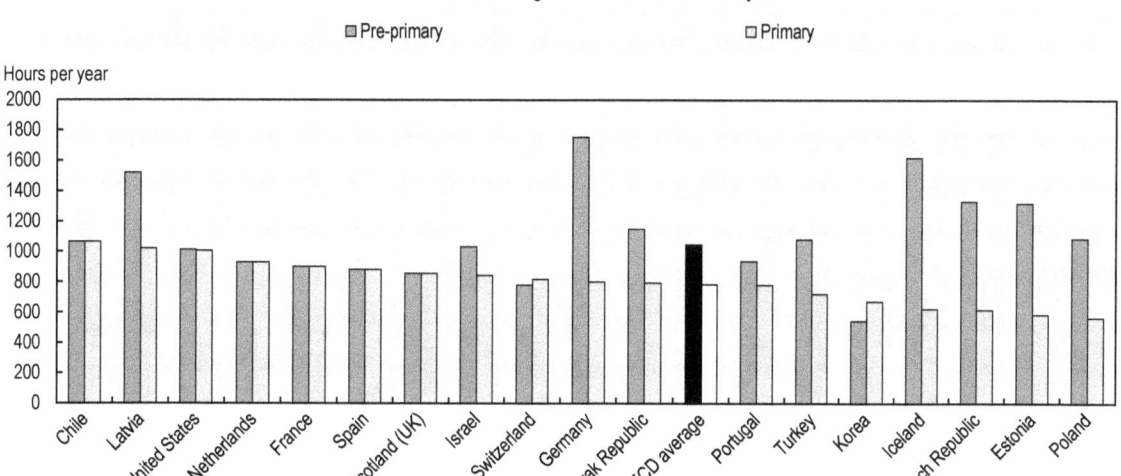

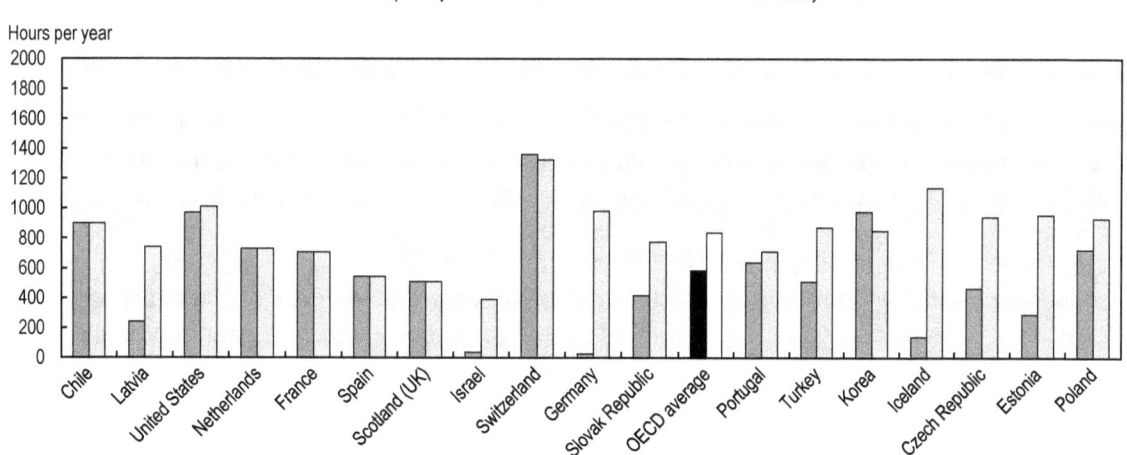

Note: For the Czech Republic, Estonia, France, Germany, Israel, Latvia, Poland, the Slovak Republic, Spain and Turkey, data refer to typical teaching time (i.e. teaching time required from most teachers when no specific circumstances apply to teachers). For Chile, the Netherlands, Portugal and Scotland (UK), maximum teaching time. For Korea, minimum teaching time. For the United actual teaching time. Data for the United States refer to 2016.
Source: OECD (2018), *Education at a Glance 2018: OECD Indicators*, https://doi.org/10.1787/19991487.

By their nature, lower child-to-staff ratios are likely to lead to increased staff costs. One option for countries with limited budgets could be introduce responsive child-to-staff regulations that adjust according to the needs and characteristics of staff and children. In England, for instance, child-to-staff ratios have been set to respond to the qualifications of staff employed in the class- and playroom. The stipulated ratio for 3- to 6-year-olds is 13 when there is a qualified teacher or equivalent in the group, but this decreases to 8 when there is no qualified teacher or equivalent present (Wall, Litjens and Taguma, 2015[36]). For 2-year-olds the minimum ratio is four children per member of staff, and for children under two it is three per member of staff. Together with Finland, England has one of the lowest child-to-staff ratios for very young children in the OECD (Wall, Litjens and Taguma, 2015[36]; Litjens and Taguma, 2017[3]).

Figure 3.3. Child-to-staff ratios in pre-primary education differ considerably across OECD countries

Average ratios of pupils to teaching staff and to all contact staff (teachers and teaching aides) in pre-primary education services (public and private), based on full-time equivalents, 2016

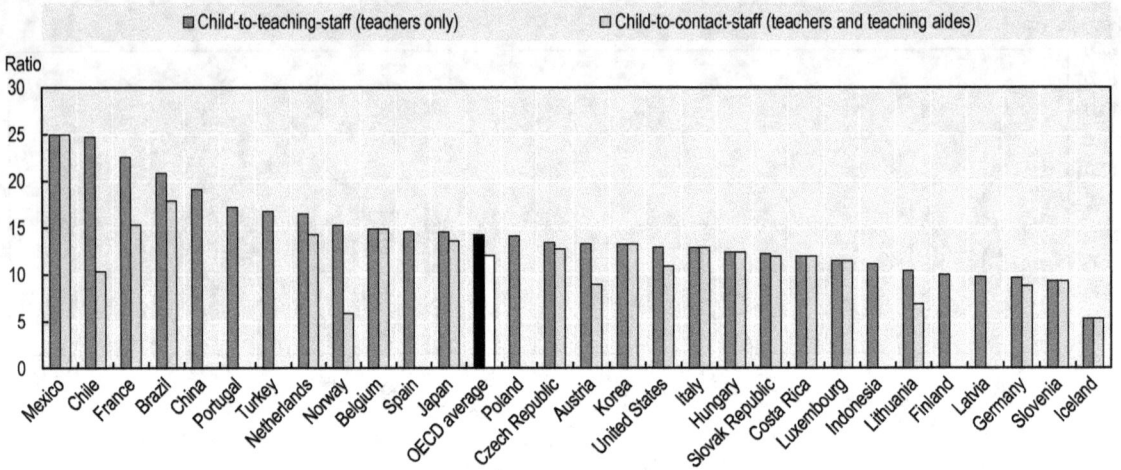

Note: Data should be interpreted with some caution since the indicator compares the teacher/student ratios in countries with '"education-only" and "integrated education and day care" programmes. In some countries, the staff requirements in these two types of provision are very different. See *OECD Education at a Glance 2018* Annex 3 for more detail (http://www.oecd.org/edu/education-at-a-glance-19991487.htm).
Source: OECD (2018[19]), *OECD Education at at Glance*, http://www.oecd.org/education/education-at-a-glance/.

Besides minimum standards, organisational features such leadership and relationships with colleagues are also important for staff retention (Litjens and Taguma, 2017[3]; Grant, Jeon and Buettner, 2019[73]). Management support, in particular, is key. Evidence shows that staff who report little support from management also express lower job satisfaction and perform their teaching and care-giving tasks less well than those who receive greater support (Ackerman, 2006[16]; Whitebook and Sakai, 2003[76]). Autonomy and independence are important too. In one study of ECEC workers in Australia, staff with a greater degree of influence and those working in settings with a flatter organisational structure often reported a stronger intention to stay (McDonald, Thorpe and Irvine, 2018[14]). Foremost among these practices was increased work-time autonomy, including control over schedules and working hours.

3.4. Encouraging in-service training and professional development

Recruiting and retaining highly qualified staff is only one part of building a high-quality workforce. Education and neuroscience is always progressing, and no matter how good the pre-service education system is, it cannot be expected to prepare ECEC staff for every challenge they will face in their careers. Existing staff need opportunities for ongoing in-service training and professional development to allow them to stay abreast of the latest advances in teaching and care practice, to update them on changes to curricula, and to help weaker staff become more effective (OECD, 2012[1]). In fact, research suggests that relevant in-service training is one of the most effective levers for process quality and for supporting children's development, learning, and well-being (OECD, 2018[2]).

In-service training may also help improve staff retention, though it is important to make a distinction here between turnover within specific centres and turnover in the wider field. Some studies find evidence that in-service training actually *increases* the likelihood of an individual leaving their specific centre, perhaps because it opens up new opportunities elsewhere inside the sector (Totenhagen et al., 2016[18]; Irvine et al., 2016[15]). There is also some danger that pressuring unwilling staff to undergo in-service training may force some workers out of their jobs (Irvine et al., 2016[15]; Bridges et al., 2011[66]). At the same time, however, training and professional development can help keep skilled workers in the ECEC sector as a whole (Totenhagen et al., 2016[18]; Irvine et al., 2016[15]). Individuals that have gained sector-specific skills through in-service training have greater incentives to remain in the field. Training and professional development can also help build professional identity and open up new career avenues, boosting commitment and career satisfaction.

In-service training and professional development activities take a variety of forms. They can be conducted "on the job" or externally – such as in colleges, universities, or other training institutions – and can be delivered through, for instance, staff meetings, workshops, conferences, subject training, field-based consultation training, supervised practices and mentoring. To be most effective, in-service training needs to be tailored to the needs of specific staff and offered on a long-term basis (OECD, 2012[1]). They key is to provide both the courses that help staff to stay abreast of the latest developments, and the training that provides staff with the tools needed to apply this knowledge in their work (OECD, 2012[1]).

A major challenge in promoting in-service training and professional development is encouraging and incentivising staff to enrol. In the absence of support, and given the low wages and poor working conditions often found in the ECEC sector, staff may feel they do not have the time or resources to attend training and professional development activities. Providers themselves may also be unwilling to let staff attend training if resources are stretched and they are not properly compensated. And there are practical considerations too – in the context of staff shortages, it may be difficult (and costly) to find substitute workers.

OECD countries have adopted a variety of measures aimed at promoting participation in in-service training and development (Litjens and Taguma, 2017[3]). In several countries, in-service training and professional development is mandatory (OECD, 2012[1]). In Slovenia, for instance, it is obligatory for teaching staff in ECEC to participate in at least five days in-service training per year, or 15 days spread across three years (Litjens and Taguma, 2017[3]; Oberhuemer and Schreyer, 2018[4]). In Austria, requirements vary across states but range from a minimum mandatory requirement for two or three days during working time to a maximum of five days during centre holidays (Oberhuemer and Schreyer, 2018[4]). In Luxembourg, most staff are obliged to attend 32 hours of professional development activities every two years, and at least eight hours annually (Oberhuemer and Schreyer, 2018[4]). In general, mandatory in-service training is more common for teachers at the pre-primary level than for staff in care-oriented services aimed at children under three (OECD, 2012[1]).

Aside from mandating training, other common strategies for encouraging staff to engage in training and professional development include financial support to cover the costs of training and earnings foregone, as well as study leave. In Slovenia, for instance, ECEC teachers undertaking in-service training receive paid study leave, plus expenses for transport costs and participation fees (Litjens and Taguma, 2017[3]). In Sweden, under the "Boost for Preschool" training programme that ran between 2009 and 2011, ECEC staff participating in university courses continued to receive 80% of their salary, with the costs shared between government and providers (Swedish Council for Higher Education, 2017[77]; Litjens and Taguma, 2017[3]). In France, public sector pre-primary teachers who have at least three years tenure have the right to a one-year job-secured professional leave, during which they continue to receive 85% of their salary. They have to submit monthly activity reports, and must commit to continuing working in the public sector for at least three times the length of the leave on their return (Oberhuemer and Schreyer, 2018[4]).

Some countries also provide cash or career incentives to staff who engage in professional development, such as wage increases or new career opportunities. In the United States, for example, several programmes and initiatives from around the country provide scholarships and wage bonuses to ECEC staff engaging in education, training and professional development (Box 3.2). Evidence suggests these kinds of programmes can help encourage staff to participate in education and training, and may also boost retention (Box 3.2). In Spain, professional development activities count as 'merits' that can be put towards eligibility for a transfer, promotion, or salary increase (Oberhuemer and Schreyer, 2018[4]). In Denmark, ECEC teachers that complete at least six weeks of professional development activities in a two-year period and pass an assessment have the opportunity to enrol in a further 'diploma study' programme, which typically provides an additional qualification in a specialised area (Oberhuemer and Schreyer, 2018[4]).

> Box 3.2. The *Teacher Education and Compensation Helps* (T.E.A.C.H.) and the *Child-care Retention Incentive* (CRI) programmes in the United States
>
> **Teacher Education and Compensation Helps (T.E.A.C.H.) programme in Wisconsin**
>
> The Teacher Education and Compensation Helps (T.E.A.C.H.) early childhood programme is a state-run initiative designed to improve the qualifications, wages, and retention of ECEC workers. The programme began in 1990 in North Carolina, but has since been introduced in other states across the United States. Today, the T.E.A.C.H programme is present in 22 states and the District of Columbia. Exact programme details vary from state to state. Here, the focus is on the implementation of T.E.A.C.H in one specific state, Wisconsin, as described in its 1999-2003 evaluation report.
>
> The T.E.A.C.H early childhood programme in Wisconsin offers scholarships to support ECEC teachers in taking college courses, and financial incentives to stay in the sector afterwards. The programme requires recipients to agree to remain in their jobs for six months to one year following completion of their contract, after which they typically receive a bonus or raise from their employer and a bonus from T.E.A.C.H. (Adams et al., 2003[78]).
>
> The primary goal of the T.E.A.C.H. early childhood programme is to support training and professional development among staff. By several measures, the 1999-2003 evaluation shows it is largely successful in this aim. Roughly half of staff receiving T.E.A.C.H. scholarships had not been in training or professional development in the year prior receipt, suggesting the programme was effective in supporting and encouraging training among staff motivated to do so. Completion rates were also high (Adams et al., 2003[78]). Three-quarters of staff awarded scholarships to study infant care courses went on to complete the course, as did 85% of those awarded scholarships for administration courses (Adams et al., 2003[78]).
>
> Improvements also extend to retention: T.E.A.C.H. recipients had an average annual turnover rate of 12%, corresponding to less than one-third the annual turnover rate across the state of Wisconsin as a whole. Even among those who left their jobs, a majority (57%) stayed in the ECEC field. Only 7.6% of recipients actually left the ECEC field altogether (Adams et al., 2003[78]). However, it is important to bear in mind that these results are based only on recipients that completed the evaluators' survey, and it is important to consider potential bias problems in the sample, as those who responded normally exhibit higher motivation and may be less likely to leave, in general.
>
> **Child-care Retention Incentive (CRI) programme in California**
>
> In 2001, California created a similar incentive programme called the Matching Funds for Child-care Retention Incentive (CRI) programme, which offered cash incentives to ECEC staff for participation in professional development. The aim was to boost staff qualification levels and reduce staff turnover. The programme spent $164 million on ECEC staff between 2001 and 2004. Local authorities were encouraged to participate through matching grants from the state (i.e. state financial contributions that "match" the funds put forward at the local level) and given the freedom to design the specific aspects of its program. The exact conditions of the grants (including who would be eligible, the intensity of

professional development activities, the level of wage incentives, and the contingency with staying in one's centre or the field) varied from one local authority to another. This feature of CRI makes it attractive option for evaluation, such as that by Bridges et al. (2011[66]), since it is possible to exploit the variability in programme characteristics in order to tease out their potentially differing effects.

One evaluation of the programme found that offering wage incentives helped encourage ECEC staff – especially lower-paid and less-senior staff – to participate in professional development courses (Bridges et al., 2011[66]). The authors report that the effect was "modest" but also consistent across sites. In terms of courses completed, lower skilled staff gained most from the intervention. Staff in more senior roles, staff who were higher paid, and staff who held greater tenure all completed fewer courses, suggesting limits to the gains for already highly qualified and/or highly paid staff. Latino assistants and staff in publicly funded ECEC centres also gained more, compared, respectively, to white assistants and staff in private fee-supported centres. It is an encouraging sign for those looking to raise average ECEC workforce credentials that lower paid staff and staff from minority populations experienced the largest gains.

Annex A. Summary of pre-service training and minimum qualification requirements

Table A.1. The length of pre-service training and minimum qualification requirements for pre-primary teachers differ considerably across countries

Minimum length of pre-service training and minimum required qualification level for teaching staff working with older children in centre-based ECEC settings, European OECD countries, 2012/13

	Minimum length of pre-service training	Minimum required qualification level
Austria	2	Post-secondary non-tertiary level
Belgium (Flemish community)	3	Bachelor's level
Belgium (French community)	3	Bachelor's level
Czech Republic	4	Upper-secondary level
Denmark	3.5	Bachelor's level
Estonia	3	Bachelor's level
Finland	3	Bachelor's level
France	5	Master's level
Germany	3	Post-secondary non-tertiary level
Greece	4	Bachelor's level
Hungary	2	Bachelor's level
Iceland	5	Master's level
Ireland	1	Post-secondary non-tertiary level
Italy	5	Master's level
Latvia	2	Post-secondary non-tertiary level
Lithuania	3	Bachelor's level
Luxembourg	4	Bachelor's level
Netherlands	..	..
Norway	3	Bachelor's level
Poland	3	Bachelor's level
Portugal	4	Master's level
Slovak Republic	4	Upper-secondary level
Slovenia	3	Bachelor's level
Spain	4	Bachelor's level
Sweden	3.5	Bachelor's level
Switzerland	3	Bachelor's level
Turkey	4	Bachelor's level
United Kingdom	..	..

Note: For Austria, initial training may either last five years (three at upper-secondary level and two at post-secondary non-tertiary level) or two years (all at post-secondary non-tertiary level).
Source: EC/EACEA/Eurydice/Eurostat (2014[38]).

References

Ackerman, D. (2006), "The Costs of Being a Child Care Teacher", *Educational Policy*, Vol. 20/1, pp. 85-112, http://dx.doi.org/10.1177/0895904805285283. [16]

Adams, D. et al. (2003), *T.E.A.C.H. Early Childhood Wisconsin Evaluation Report*, Wisconsin Child Care Research Partnership, University of Wisconsin, http://www.uwex.edu/ces/flp/ece/wccrp.html (accessed on 14 January 2019). [78]

BLS (2017), *National Occupational Employment and Wage Estimates*, https://www.bls.gov/oes/2017/may/oes_nat.htm#39-0000 (accessed on 6 February 2019). [30]

Bonetti, S. (2019), *The Early Years Workforce in England: A comparative analysis using the Labour Force Survey*, Education Policy Institute, https://epi.org.uk/wp-content/uploads/2019/01/The-early-years-workforce-in-England_EPI.pdf (accessed on 6 February 2019). [31]

Bridges, M. et al. (2011), "Strengthening the Early Childhood Workforce: How Wage Incentives May Boost Training and Job Stability", *Early Education & Development*, Vol. 22/6, pp. 1009-1029, http://dx.doi.org/10.1080/10409289.2010.514537. [66]

Brind, R. et al. (2014), "Childcare and Early Years Providers Survey 2013", *TNS BMRB Report*, No. JN 117328, Department for Education, https://assets.publishing.service.gov.uk/government/uploads/system/uploads/attachment_data/file/355075/SFR33_2014_Main_report.pdf (accessed on 14 January 2019). [52]

Ceeda (2018), *About Early Years: The independent sector research programme: Annual report 2017/18*, http://aboutearlyyears.co.uk/ReportDownload/DownloadReport/970610b2-526d-46f0-ab2b-a6670e890f1b?guid=9662cd37-d351-4eb8-b74c-745ec4482a00 (accessed on 6 February 2019). [21]

Destatis (2018), *Kinder und tätige Personen in Tageseinrichtungen und in öffentlich geförderter Kindertagespflege am 01.03.2018*, Statistisches Bundesamt, https://www.destatis.de/DE/Publikationen/Thematisch/Soziales/KinderJugendhilfe/TageseinrichtungenKindertagespflege.html (accessed on 28 February 2019). [8]

DfE (2019), *Get Into Teaching*, https://getintoteaching.education.gov.uk/ (accessed on 9 February 2019). [29]

DfE (2018), *Childcare and Early Years Providers Survey: 2018*, Department for Education, https://www.gov.uk/government/statistics/childcare-and-early-years-providers-survey-2018 (accessed on 8 February 2019). [25]

DfE (2018), *Initial Teacher Training (ITT) Census for the academic year 2018 to 2019, England*, Department for Education, https://assets.publishing.service.gov.uk/government/uploads/system/uploads/attachment_data/file/759716/ITT_Census_2018_to_2019_main_text.pdf (accessed on 6 February 2019). [22]

DfE (2018), *Survey of Childcare and Early Years Providers: Main Summary, England, 2018*, Department for Education, https://assets.publishing.service.gov.uk/government/uploads/system/uploads/attachment_data/file/752919/Survey_of_Childcare_and_Early_Years_Providers_2018_Main_Summary3.pdf (accessed on 14 January 2019). [56]

DoET (2017), *Recognition of Prior Learning (RPL) Assessment Toolkits*, Department of Education and Training, https://www.education.gov.au/recognition-prior-learning-rpl-assessment-toolkits (accessed on 8 February 2019). [26]

EC/EACEA/Eurydice/Eurostat (2014), *Key Data on Early Childhood Education and Care in Europe: 2014 Edition*, Publications Office of the European Union, Luxembourg, http://dx.doi.org/10.2797/75270. [38]

Engel, A. et al. (2015), *Early Childhood Education and Care Policy Review: Norway*, OECD, Paris, http://www.oecd.org/norway/Early-Childhood-Education-and-Care-Policy-Review-Norway.pdf (accessed on 14 January 2019). [9]

Eurydice (2019), *Eurydice Database*, https://eacea.ec.europa.eu/national-policies/eurydice/home_en (accessed on 8 March 2019). [40]

Gable, S. et al. (2007), "Cash incentives and turnover in center-based child care staff", *Early Childhood Research Quarterly*, Vol. 22/3, pp. 363-378, http://dx.doi.org/10.1016/J.ECRESQ.2007.06.002. [71]

Grant, A., L. Jeon and C. Buettner (2019), "Relating early childhood teachers' working conditions and well-being to their turnover intentions", *Educational Psychology*, pp. 1-19, http://dx.doi.org/10.1080/01443410.2018.1543856. [73]

Hadfield, M. et al. (2012), "Longitudinal Study of Early Years Professional Status: an exploration of progress, leadership and impact: Final report", *Research Report*, No. DFE-RR239c, Department for Education, https://assets.publishing.service.gov.uk/government/uploads/system/uploads/attachment_data/file/183418/DfE-RR239c_report.pdf (accessed on 14 January 2019). [53]

Hale-Jinks, C., H. Knopf and H. Knopf (2006), "Tackling Teacher Turnover in Child Care: Understanding Causes and Consequences, Identifying Solutions", *Childhood Education*, Vol. 82/4, pp. 219-226, http://dx.doi.org/10.1080/00094056.2006.10522826. [68]

Hall, D. and B. Langton (2006), *Perceptions of the Status of Teachers*, Ministry of Education New Zealand, http://www.minedu.govt.nz/index.cfm?layout=document&documentid=11171&data=l&goto=00 (accessed on 8 February 2019). [23]

IfD-Allensbach (2018), *Erziehen als Beruf: Wahrnehmungen der Bevölkerung zum Berufsfeld Erzieherin/Erzieher*, Institut für Demoskopie Allensbach, https://www.bmfsfj.de/blob/131410/6ab4e834086a8fbc8e0acf4b8343d7d3/allensbach-studie-2018--erzieher-beruf--data.pdf (accessed on 27 February 2019). [13]

Irvine, S. et al. (2016), *Money, Love and Identity: Initial Findings from the National ECEC Workforce Study*, https://eprints.qut.edu.au/101622/1/Brief_report_ECEC_Workforce_Development_Policy_Workshop_final.pdf (accessed on 15 January 2019). [15]

Jensen, J. (2017), *DENMARK ECEC Workforce Profile - SEEPRO*, http://www.seepro.eu/English/Country_Reports.htm (accessed on 18 February 2019). [64]

Karlsson Lohmander, M. (2017), "Sweden – ECEC Workforce Profile", in Oberhuemer, P. and I. Schreyer (eds.), *Workforce Profiles in Systems of Early Childhood Education and Care in Europe,*, http://www.seepro.eu/English/Country_Reports.htm (accessed on 14 January 2019). [33]

KD (2017), *Kompetanse for Fremtidens Barnehage:; Revidert Strategi for Kompetanse og Rekruttering 2018–2022*, Kunnskapsdepartementet, https://www.regjeringen.no/contentassets/7e72a90a6b884d0399d9537cce8b801e/kompetansestrategi-for-barnehage-2018_2022.pdf (accessed on 8 March 2019). [42]

Lange, J. (2017), *Leitung von Kindertageseinrichtungen: Eine Bestandsaufnahme von Leitungskräften und Leitungsstrukturen in Deutschland*, Bertelsmann Stiftung, Gütersloh, https://www.laendermonitor.de/fileadmin/files/BSt/Publikationen/GrauePublikationen/Leitung_von_Kindertageseinrichtungen.pdf (accessed on 8 March 2019). [41]

Lärarförbundet (2018), *Fast track: opportunity for newly arrived teachers*, https://www.lararforbundet.se/artiklar/fast-track-opportunity-for-newly-arrived-teachers-5746935c-ff1d-4611-913b-7cc9336ff593 (accessed on 13 February 2019). [50]

Litjens, I. and M. Taguma (2017), *Early childhood education and care staff recruitment and retention: A review for Kazakhstan*, OECD, https://www.oecd.org/education/school/Early-Childhood-Education-and-Care-Staff-Recruitement-Retention-Kazakhstan.pdf (accessed on 14 January 2019). [3]

Manlove, E. and J. Guzell (1997), "Intention to leave, anticipated reasons for leaving, and 12-month turnover of child care center staff", *Early Childhood Research Quarterly*, Vol. 12/2, pp. 145-167, http://dx.doi.org/10.1016/S0885-2006(97)90010-7. [72]

Martin, C. and D. Ruble (2010), "Patterns of gender development.", *Annual review of psychology*, Vol. 61, pp. 353-81, http://dx.doi.org/10.1146/annurev.psych.093008.100511. [62]

Martin, C. and D. Ruble (2004), "Children's Search for Gender Cues", *Current Directions in Psychological Science*, Vol. 13/2, pp. 67-70, http://dx.doi.org/10.1111/j.0963-7214.2004.00276.x. [61]

Mathers, S. et al. (2011), "Evaluation of the Graduate Leader Fund: Final report", *Research Report*, No. DFE-RR144, Department for Education, https://assets.publishing.service.gov.uk/government/uploads/system/uploads/attachment_data/file/181480/DFE-RR144.pdf (accessed on 14 January 2019). [54]

McDonald, P., K. Thorpe and S. Irvine (2018), "Low pay but still we stay: Retention in early childhood education and care", *Journal of Industrial Relations*, Vol. 60/5, pp. 647-668, http://dx.doi.org/10.1177/0022185618800351. [14]

Meade, A. et al. (2012), *Early Childhood Teachers' Work in Education and Care Centres: Profiles, Patterns and Purposes*, Te Tari Puna Ora o Aotearoa/New Zealand Childcare Association, Wellington,, https://ecnz.ac.nz/assets/RelatedDocuments/Early-Childhood-Teachers-work-in-education-and-carecentres-web-090812.pdf. [44]

Mitchell, L. et al. (2011), *Locality-based evaluation of Pathways to the Future: Ngā Huarahi Arataki*, Ministry of Education New Zealand, http://www.waikato.ac.nz (accessed on 7 February 2019). [43]

MoE (2019), *Education Counts: Early Child Education Staffing Statistics*, https://www.educationcounts.govt.nz/statistics/early-childhood-education/staffing (accessed on 7 February 2019). [46]

MoE (2019), *Education in New Zealand*, http://www.education.govt.nz/ (accessed on 9 February 2019). [28]

MoE (2019), *TeachNZ Early Childhood Education Scholarships*, https://www.teachnz.govt.nz/studying-to-be-a-teacher/scholarships/teachnz-early-childhood-education-scholarships/ (accessed on 10 February 2019). [35]

MoE (2018), *Recognising prior learning in ECE study*, Ministry of Education New Zealand, https://www.education.govt.nz/early-childhood/employment/working-in-ece/recognising-prior-learning/ (accessed on 8 February 2019). [27]

MoE (2014), *Teachers in early childhood education*, https://www.educationcounts.govt.nz/statistics/archived/ece2/ece-indicators/54190 (accessed on 27 February 2019). [12]

MoE (2013), *Annual ECE Census: Report 2013*, https://www.educationcounts.govt.nz/publications/series/annual-early-childhood-education-census (accessed on 13 February 2019). [47]

MoE (2008), *State of Education in New Zealand 2008*, Ministry of Education, http://www.educationcounts.govt.nz (accessed on 7 February 2019). [45]

Moloney, M. (2015), "A vocation or a career: the perspectives of BA. ECEC graduates about accessing employment and working in the early years sector in Ireland", *Irish Educational Studies*, Vol. 34/4, pp. 325-339, http://dx.doi.org/10.1080/03323315.2015.1119705. [11]

National Apprenticeship Service (2018), *A guide to apprenticeships*, Skills Funding Agency, https://assets.publishing.service.gov.uk/government/uploads/system/uploads/attachment_data/file/699397/Guide-to-Apprenticeships_090418.pdf (accessed on 18 February 2019). [49]

National Apprenticeship Service (2018), *A-Z of apprenticeships*, Skills Funding Agency, https://assets.publishing.service.gov.uk/government/uploads/system/uploads/attachment_data/file/699398/Apps_Framesworks-090418.pdf (accessed on 18 February 2019). [48]

Nutbrown, C. (2012), *Foundations for Quality: The independent review of early education and childcare qualifications: Final Report*, Department for Education, https://assets.publishing.service.gov.uk/government/uploads/system/uploads/attachment_data/file/175463/Nutbrown-Review.pdf (accessed on 14 January 2019). [55]

Oberhuemer, P. (2011), "The Early Childhood Education Workforce in Europe Between Divergencies and Emergencies", *International Journal of Child Care and Education Policy*, Vol. 5/1, pp. 55-63, http://dx.doi.org/10.1007/2288-6729-5-1-55. [60]

Oberhuemer, P. and I. Schreyer (eds.) (2018), *Early Childhood Workforce Profiles in 30 Countries with Key Contextual Data*, http://www.seepro.eu/English/Country_Reports.htm (accessed on 14 January 2019). [4]

OECD (2018), *Education at a Glance 2018: OECD Indicators*, OECD Publishing, Paris, https://dx.doi.org/10.1787/eag-2018-en. [19]

OECD (2018), *Engaging Young Children: Lessons from Research about Quality in Early Childhood Education and Care*, Starting Strong, OECD Publishing, Paris, https://dx.doi.org/10.1787/9789264085145-en. [2]

OECD (2018), *OECD Family Database*, http://www.oecd.org/els/family/database.htm (accessed on 20 April 2018). [6]

OECD (2017), *Starting Strong 2017: Key OECD Indicators on Early Childhood Education and Care*, Starting Strong, OECD Publishing, Paris, https://dx.doi.org/10.1787/9789264276116-en. [5]

OECD (2017), *Starting Strong V: Transitions from Early Childhood Education and Care to Primary Education*, Starting Strong, OECD Publishing, Paris, https://dx.doi.org/10.1787/9789264276253-en. [32]

OECD (2017), *The Pursuit of Gender Equality: An Uphill Battle*, OECD Publishing, Paris, https://dx.doi.org/10.1787/9789264281318-en. [63]

OECD (2014), *Education at a Glance 2014: OECD Indicators*, OECD Publishing, Paris, https://dx.doi.org/10.1787/eag-2014-en. [24]

OECD (2012), *Starting strong III : a quality toolbox for early childhood education and care.*, OECD. [1]

OECD (2001), *Starting Strong*, Starting Strong, OECD Publishing, Paris, https://dx.doi.org/10.1787/9789264276116-en. [37]

Peeters, J. (2007), *Including Men in Early Childhood Education: Insights from the European Experience*, http://www.stop4-7.be/files/includingmenineartlychildhoodeducation.pdf (accessed on 14 January 2019). [58]

Peeters, J., T. Rohrmann and K. Emilsen (2015), "Gender balance in ECEC: why is there so little progress?", *European Early Childhood Education Research Journal*, Vol. 23/3, pp. 302-314, http://dx.doi.org/10.1080/1350293X.2015.1043805. [59]

Pramling-Samuelsson, I. et al. (2016), "Swedish preschool teachers' ideas of the ideal preschool group", *Journal of Early Childhood Research*, Vol. 14/4, pp. 444-460, http://dx.doi.org/10.1177/1476718X14559233. [75]

Press, F., S. Wong and M. Gibson (2015), "Journal of Family Studies Understanding who cares: creating the evidence to address the long-standing policy problem of staff shortages in early childhood education and care", *Journal of Family Studies*, Vol. 21/1, pp. 87-100, http://dx.doi.org/10.1080/13229400.2015.1020990. [10]

Prognos (2018), *Zukunftsszenarien: Fachkräfte in der Frühen Bildung gewinnen und binden*, Prognos AG, Berlin, https://www.dji.de/fileadmin/user_upload/bibs2017/rauschenbach_schilling_plaetze_personal_finanzen.pdf (accessed on 25 February 2019). [7]

Schreyer, I. and M. Krause (2016), "Pedagogical staff in children's day care centres in Germany – links between working conditions, job satisfaction, commitment and work-related stress", *Early Years: An International Research Journal*, Vol. 36/2, pp. 132-147, http://dx.doi.org/10.1080/09575146.2015.1115390. [74]

Schreyer, I. et al. (2014), *AQUA: Arbeitsplatz und Qualität in Kitas. Ergebnisse einer bundesweiten Befragung*, Staatsinstitut für Frühpädagogik, München, http://www.aqua-studie.de (accessed on 10 March 2019). [17]

SSB (2019), *StatBank Norway*, https://www.ssb.no/en/statbank (accessed on 14 January 2019). [65]

Statskontoret (2017), *Utvärdering av statsbidrag för lärarlönelyftet: Delrapport 1*, Statskontoret, Stockholm, http://www.statskontoret.se (accessed on 7 February 2019). [34]

Sumsion, J. (2005), "Male teachers in early childhood education: issues and case study", *Early Childhood Research Quarterly*, Vol. 20/1, pp. 109-123, http://dx.doi.org/10.1016/J.ECRESQ.2005.01.001. [57]

Swedish Council for Higher Education (2017), *Follow up and evaluation of experimental work with exercise schools and training nurseries within teacher and pre-school training*. [77]

Sylva, K. et al. (2010), *Early childhood matters: Evidence from the effective pre-school and primary education project*, Routledge, https://doi.org/10.4324/9780203862063. [51]

Sylva, K. et al. (eds.) (2010), *Early Childhood Matters: Evidence from the Effective Pre-school and Primary Education Project*, Routledge, http://dx.doi.org/10.4324/9780203862063. [39]

T.E.A.C.H Early Childhood National Center (2017), *Child Care WAGE$ Initiative Overview*, T.E.A.C.H Early Childhood National Center, https://teachecnationalcenter.org/wp-content/uploads/2014/10/WAGES_overview_FactSht_9_25_18v4.pdf (accessed on 15 February 2019). [70]

Thorpe, K. et al. (2011), "Who wants to work in childcare? pre-service early childhood teacher's consideration of work in the child-care sector", *Australasian Journal of Early Childhood*, https://epubs.scu.edu.au/educ_pubs/418 (accessed on 15 January 2019). [20]

Totenhagen, C. et al. (2016), "Retaining Early Childhood Education Workers: A Review of the Empirical Literature", *Journal of Research in Childhood Education*, Vol. 30/4, pp. 585-599, http://dx.doi.org/10.1080/02568543.2016.1214652. [18]

Wall, S., I. Litjens and M. Taguma (2015), *Early Childhood Education and Care Review: England*, OECD Publishing, Paris, http://www.oecd.org/education/school/early-childhood-education-and-care-pedagogy-review-england.pdf (accessed on 13 January 2019). [36]

Wells, M. (2015), "Predicting preschool teacher retention and turnover in newly hired Head Start teachers across the first half of the school year", *Early Childhood Research Quarterly*, Vol. 30, pp. 152-159, http://dx.doi.org/10.1016/j.ecresq.2014.10.003. [67]

Wells, M. (2015), "Predicting preschool teacher retention and turnover in newly hired Head Start teachers across the first half of the school year", *Early Childhood Research Quarterly*, Vol. 30, pp. 152-159, http://dx.doi.org/10.1016/J.ECRESQ.2014.10.003. [69]

Whitebook, M. and L. Sakai (2003), "Turnover begets turnover: an examination of job and occupational instability among child care center staff", *Early Childhood Research Quarterly*, Vol. 18/3, pp. 273-293, http://dx.doi.org/10.1016/S0885-2006(03)00040-1. [76]

Wohlfahrt Intern (2019), *So zahlt die Sozialwirtschaft: Jahrbuch Tarif und Entgelt 2019*, Röthig Medien, Berlin. [79]

Notes

[1] "Process quality" refers to the proximal processes that affect children's everyday experiences in ECEC, such as the quality of teacher-child interactions and development activities and the quality of child-to-child (peer) interactions (OECD, 2018[2]). It is distinct from structural quality – the other main determinant of overall quality – which refers to factors such as infrastructure and physical setting (OECD, 2018[2]). For me detail on the importance of process quality for child development, learning and well-being, see OECD (2018[2]).

[2] Although teachers attaining qualified teacher status through primary education initial teacher training can also work in ECEC settings if they wish, and some entrants planning on a career in ECEC may choose this route to qualification.

[3] In January 2019, according to one summary of 40 collective agreements, the gross basic starting salary of a pre-primary teacher ("Erzieher") ranged from EUR 27 100 to EUR 38 700, depending on the relevant agreement (Wohlfahrt Intern, 2019[79]).

[4] Figures from 2014 onwards are not comparable due to a change in data collection, but in absolute terms the number of qualified and registered teachers in teacher-led ECEC services has continued to increase since (MoE, 2019[46]).

ORGANISATION FOR ECONOMIC CO-OPERATION AND DEVELOPMENT

The OECD is a unique forum where governments work together to address the economic, social and environmental challenges of globalisation. The OECD is also at the forefront of efforts to understand and to help governments respond to new developments and concerns, such as corporate governance, the information economy and the challenges of an ageing population. The Organisation provides a setting where governments can compare policy experiences, seek answers to common problems, identify good practice and work to co-ordinate domestic and international policies.

The OECD member countries are: Australia, Austria, Belgium, Canada, Chile, the Czech Republic, Denmark, Estonia, Finland, France, Germany, Greece, Hungary, Iceland, Ireland, Israel, Italy, Japan, Korea, Latvia, Lithuania, Luxembourg, Mexico, the Netherlands, New Zealand, Norway, Poland, Portugal, the Slovak Republic, Slovenia, Spain, Sweden, Switzerland, Turkey, the United Kingdom and the United States. The European Union takes part in the work of the OECD.

OECD Publishing disseminates widely the results of the Organisation's statistics gathering and research on economic, social and environmental issues, as well as the conventions, guidelines and standards agreed by its members.

OECD PUBLISHING, 2, rue André-Pascal, 75775 PARIS CEDEX 16
ISBN 978-92-64-89724-3 – 2019

www.ingramcontent.com/pod-product-compliance
Lightning Source LLC
LaVergne TN
LVHW061957070526
838199LV00060B/4174